D1091310

COLLECTED POEMS

John Reed

COLLECTED POEMS

EDITED AND WITH A FOREWORD
BY CORLISS LAMONT

LAWRENCE HILL & COMPANY
Westport, Connecticut

ACKNOWLEDGMENTS

The publishers acknowledge with thanks the permission of the Rare Book and Manuscript Library of Columbia University to publish this collection drawn from the manuscript of the Master's Essay prepared by Leo Stoller at Columbia University in 1947. We also wish to thank Mr. Stoller's wife, Constance Stoller, for her kind cooperation.

Published in the United States by Lawrence Hill & Company,
520 Riverside Avenue, Westport, Connecticut 06880

Manufactured in the United States of America

Library of Congress Cataloging in Publication Data

Reed, John, 1887–1920.
  Collected poems.

  I. Lamont, Corliss, 1902-   . II. Title.
PS3535.E2786A17   1985   811'.52   82-48442
ISBN 0-88208-189-6

Contents

Foreword

Soon after I entered Harvard College in the Class of 1924, I heard about a famous member of the Class of 1910, John Reed (1887-1920), with classmates such as columnist Walter Lippmann, painter Robert Hallowell and psychiatrist Carl Binger. After I read Reed's *Ten Days That Shook the World,* admittedly the best eye-witness account of the 1917 Communist Revolution in Russia, I became increasingly interested in his adventurous career. Thinking that the Harvard community did not fully appreciate him, I later organized a Harvard Alumni John Reed Committee that commissioned Hallowell to paint Reed's portrait. Hallowell did a splendid job in oils on glass, and the portrait has hung for many years in Adams House at Harvard. The committee also persuaded Granville Hicks to write his excellent biography, *John Reed: The Making of a Revolutionary.*

Meanwhile, I had become associated with Columbia University as a student (Ph.D.), teacher and currently Seminar Associate. I also worked closely with Columbia's Rare Book and Manuscript Library, of which Kenneth A. Lohf is the able and discerning librarian. Now and then I helped with some of that library's special collections. On one occasion, checking through some old manuscripts and other materials, I came across a somewhat battered, black, loose-leaf notebook. When I opened the cover, I was astonished to read, "The Collected Verse of John Reed, submitted by Leo Stoller in partial fulfillment of the requirements for the degree of Master of Arts, Faculty of Philosophy, Columbia University, June, 1947."

I had been vaguely aware that Reed had written some poetry, but to my knowledge it had never been collected in one volume. I felt that perhaps I had made a literary discovery. Thinking it over for a while, I decided that this unknown Master's Essay, hidden away in Columbia's archives, should be published to round out the dramatic story of John Reed. And I am happy that this is finally taking place.

Dr. Leo Stoller (1921-68), whose originality in research led to the collecting of Reed's poems, later obtained his Ph.D. at Columbia with a thesis on Henry David Thoreau. This was published under the title of *After Walden* by the Stanford University Press. Professor Stoller went on to become a teacher of American literature at the University of New Hampshire, Indiana University and Wayne State University. We are grateful to him for his painstaking and perceptive introduction.

John Reed, who died in Moscow from typhus a few days before his thirty-third birthday, had built up a distinguished record as a reporter in the years preceding and during the First World War, and became widely acknowledged as the outstanding American war correspondent. At the same time there was a constant note of idealism in his dispatches and a profound sympathy for the underdog everywhere. As Max Lerner put it, Reed's brief life turned out to be "one of the most deadly serious attempts ever made by an American to organize his experience into something that had meaning and stature."

Yet side by side with his zestful reporting, and not generally known, Reed had a strong poetic urge. In fact, his first literary efforts were in the realm of poetry. Upon Reed's death Louis Untermeyer wrote: "He was an idealist who combined boisterous humor and a quiet passion for truth...I remember him as the invincible romantic, the poet-satirist...the exuberant champion of a day to come when it will be possible for poets to challenge and perhaps change the world with their vision."

Despite the tumultuous action and varied scenery in so short a life—allying himself with the IWW (International Workers of the World), writing for the historic *Masses,* riding with Pancho Villa in the Mexican Revolution, imprisoned in Finland, witnessing the Russian Revolution—John Reed kept writing poetry throughout those years to record his feelings about the events and passions of his time that moved him most deeply.

Collected Poems ranges from his youthful period, when he was composing forceful poetry for student publications, to the time of his maturity—when he became, as George Kennan said, "a poet of the first order"—including his satire on Greenwich Village, "The Day in Bohemia"; his long major work "America 1918"; and the lyrical "A

Letter to Louise [Bryant]," his last poem. Untermeyer called Reed "the most vivid figure of the period."

This volume of verse reveals special aspects of the author's character and talents, showing a little known side of his cultural development and aspirations. The book underlines the tragedy of this dynamo of a man dying in the prime of life, an event that cut short the promise of other notable achievements. I have ever deeply mourned John Reed's untimely death.

Corliss Lamont □
March, 1985

Introduction

When John Reed was arrested during the Paterson silk-workers' strike, the court recorder asked him his occupation; Reed answered "Poet." Even as a schoolboy he had "felt sure" he was "going to be a great poet and novelist." His novels survive in manuscript as plot outlines. For more than a generation his published verse has rested unread in the dustier issues of contemporary magazines and in a few volumes scattered among the old-book dealers. The faces of even those few who know him as a radical journalist show genuine astonishment at the information that he once considered himself primarily a poet. Resurrected, the verses reflect directly the man's truncated development. Dying tragically, just over the threshold of his long postponed maturity, he had failed to express that maturity in verse.

John Reed was born in Portland, Oregon, in 1887, grandson to one of the city's leading industrialists. Led carefully in the path of upper-class youth, he was educated in private schools and then sent east to Harvard, where his distinction was neither in scholarship nor in radical thought but in pranks and the leading of football cheers. Following his graduation with the notable class of 1910, he toured Europe as a young adventurer whose escapades rapidly filtered back into American gossip. When he returned home, anxious "to make a million dollars," he did not differ from many another well-to-do contemporary who had fully enjoyed a wild youth and was now settling down to achieve the American dream of success.

But in John Reed two forces soon became apparent, fighting (within and without him) for control of his life. Both can undoubtedly be traced to his earlier years, but each was set into distinct motion by Lincoln Steffens. As a friend of Reed's father, he had been entrusted with the young man's guardianship in New York with the express purpose of allowing him to develop into a poet. Steffens got Reed a job on *The American Magazine,* starting him on a journalistic career which in a few years made Reed one of the most popular and best paid reporters in America.

Steffens also introduced Reed to radicals and radical thought, in particular to the I.W.W., starting him on a strange journey that eventually ended in a grave by the Kremlin wall. These two forces and their adjuncts, those of success and romance and those of poverty and radicalism, were opposed within Reed's personality; but it was their mutual intersection which produced the short-lived victory of one over the other. Reed's steps to success in journalism proved also to be steps toward Communism. Malcolm Cowley claims that Reed "became a revolutionist for reasons that were both profound and fundamentally literary. He could write supremely well on only one subject—on men revolting against the institutions that prevented them from leading human lives."

It was journalistic ability that sent him to Mexico to experience the fundamental emotion of men in just rebellion, to the scene of the Ludlow massacre to witness the horrors of military repression, to Europe to learn that war which is attractively romantic when fought for a just cause is terrifyingly repulsive when fought for markets, to Russia to participate in a rebellion by men who fought for a just cause against a repressive government which supported a war for markets. Having returned from Russia he stood trial for his opposition to the First World War, took a leading part in the organization of the American Communist Party, and died while on a mission for that party in Moscow, where he succeeded in affiliating it with the Third International. This was the Pilgrim's Progress of a Communist, although what in blocked outline appears to be a balanced story of internal conflict and final victory was in reality a complex spiritual warfare dotted with defeats and retreats and ending with the enemy conquered but not entirely obliterated.

Reed's life, approaching in surge and proportion that of a legendary hero, challenged his generation and its children to bring it within the grasp of their philosophies. As these people divided in social position, in political ideology, and in personal constitution they divided on John Reed. The mark of this fission was their attitude to Reed's own conflict between reality and romance.

Romance for John Reed meant the escapades of a Harvard graduate in Europe, the passionate loves of a Greenwich Village bohemian, the amazing success story of a young journalist; reality meant opposition to the First World War, support of the Bolsheviks in Russia, and the organization of Communists in America. If Reed was to be a hero but not a radical hero, his politics must be attacked, his poetry and adventure overpraised.

Knowingly or innocently, this was the tactic adopted by Walter Lippmann in 1914 when he called Reed "a person who enjoys himself...one of the intractables, to whom the organized monotony and virtue of our civilization are unbearable," and continued in a straight line to *Time's* comment in 1936 that Reed "was a Promethean playboy and what he played with was fire." Aided by occasional representatives of the left who picked up the phrase "playboy of the social revolution," those commentators wrote that Reed was an "eternal amateur" always "bartering all else for some adventurous need"; that he was a poet whose art had curdled to propaganda when he espoused radicalism; that he had "come to hate present society out of sheer *ennui*" and "liked the revolution [because] it was so different, so much more exciting than [he] had at any time dreamed."

The most ambitious attempt in this direction was undoubtedly Julian Street's article in *The Saturday Evening Post*, "A Soviet Saint—The Story of John Reed." Street very much liked the young Reed who had come to New York after graduation from Harvard and a trip to Europe, "tall, broad-shouldered, restless, eager, talented, perverse and disputatious,...the embodiment of sparkling and audacious youth." He finds room in his article for all the popular stories about this youth who "sought adventure everywhere"—how Reed, sailing for Europe, was arrested for murder when his friend leaped off the deck and swam ashore; how Reed paraded through Paris wearing one red and one black stocking, knickers, and an enormous cowboy hat; how Reed travelled with thieves who stole his watch and stayed with them another night to steal it back. He quotes from "The Day in Bohemia"and tells about the play Reed wrote for the exclusive Dutch Treat Club. "In whatever he did he dramatized himself, and as poets are traditionally underfed, Jack, faithful to his role, sometimes did a little amateur starving." With an unsubstantiated tale like the last and with others quite well documented, Street builds up the image of the young, handsome, adventurous, lovable—if somewhat egotistical—poet. The villain of the piece is Lincoln Steffens. Through him, says

Street, Reed met "a labor agitator and other radicals of various hues."

Opposing Lippmann and Street, radicals of the postwar decade found in John Reed a hero for their own class and ideology. He became their "captain" and they soldiers who would "raise John Reed's banner in the thickest of the strife"; he became the giant from the West who had arrived "with new voices, with a new song," and for Clarence Darrow "one of the rarest and most devoted men who ever laid down his life for a noble dream." The force which led their opponents to attack Reed's politics and praise his bohemianism led them to praise his politics and slight or omit his bohemianism.

Characteristic of this distortion from the left is the introduction written by Albert Rhys Williams to a Russian edition of *Ten Days That Shook the World.* Here are no anecdotes about escapades in France and Spain, no hint of the life of Greenwich Village. Reed's radicalism is traced to the militancy of his father who, as a United States marshal, had fought lumber kings in the far Northwest. His career at Harvard is undeservedly crowned with the organization of the Socialist Club "right in the centre of this stronghold of plutocracy." His trip to Europe after graduation and his escape to Italy after the Paterson Pageant are left unmentioned.

Neither distortion from the left nor distortion from the right could recreate a complete John Reed. It is, however, to the work of a radical scholar, Granville Hicks, and a radical writer, John Stuart, that we are indebted for *John Reed: The Making of a Revolutionary* (1936), the first genuine attempt to see in their proper relation the romance and reality of Reed's life, a life since described by Max Lerner as "one of the most deadly serious attempts ever made by an American to organize his experience into something that had meaning and stature." The path by which Reed attained this truest maturity seen by Lerner was warped into curves and twists by the clutch of opposing forces.

These forces took the surface forms of wealth and fame, poverty and ostracism, writing popularly for much money, writing unpopularly for a pittance, writing prose, writing verse, but they and the corresponding powers drawn from within Reed reflect with deep truth essential conflicts which now cleave our society and its conscious members. When John Reed chose to fight for the common people instead of deserting them for a life of private bohemianism, and when he had perforce to choose the manner in which this fight was to be conducted and the weapons with which to arm himself, he made a decision and faced a problem which have been the central experiences of many thinking men in the generation since his death. Reed was not a systematic thinker; when he had grasped a truth it was only after uncertainty and painful groping.

The contrasts of his life are the workings of the search for truth as John Reed experienced it: the member of the Harvard Club of New York is also a member of the International Workers of the World; the writer for popular magazines sends his best articles to *The Masses;* the organizer of the Paterson Pageant runs away with a rich mistress to Italy; the best war correspondent opposes the World War; the journalist who could name his own price within normal political boundaries goes outside them to Communism and relative poverty. To a lesser degree, the conflict is expressed in his poetry. The very fact that his output of verse rapidly declined as his radicalism deepened is a measure of this conflict, for Reed's poetry tended and at times was intended to express his romanticism. Within the group of poems left by Reed and here for the first time collected, the gradual resolution of the conflict within the poet is the unifying thread.

Fully half of Reed's poems were written while he attended the Morristown School in New Jersey and Harvard College, a period between his seventeenth and twenty-third birthdays. These poems divide themselves into two groups: the humorous, written for *The Harvard Lampoon,* and the serious, written for various other school and college periodicals. And though his verse ranges from quip and limerick to doggerel narrative, Reed does not outgrow his situation, but gives us poems of the same wit as had been printed in *Lampoon's* earlier years and are to be expected in any similar college magazine. Two long poems and a short song celebrate the athletic rivalry between Harvard and Yale; others jibe at the shivering "members of a famous dormitory crew," at the freshman learning to smoke a pipe, and at the college poet's annual spring "flood of ...impassioned verse." For the medical school he writes a song whose lightheartedness is in grim contrast to the "Hospital Notes" written later after he had himself been on the operating table. The humorous strain so prominent in the younger Reed was a casualty to the earnest severity of the revolutionary, and those who most opposed Reed's politics were its chief mourners.

Reed's serious school and college poems include those on expected adolescent themes, but as a group they exhibit an attitude toward life which Reed later recognized when he wrote that in New York he "first saw that reality transcended all the fine poetic invention of fastidiousness and mediaevalism." Romantic nature and the romantic past dominate these poems. His absorption in the romantic past transformed the adolescent's girl friends into symbols of Arthurian damsels and himself on the Morristown football field into a knight for whom the Sangraal hovered in the sky above the gridiron. In his poems, southern California becomes interesting because of its ancient Spanish inhabitants. For Reed the past meant largely King Arthur; and Tennyson, the celebrator of the Round Table, logically became Reed's earliest poetic hero, addressed in these words:

> Singer of the kingly Arthur,
>> Deathless song which cannot die,
> To thy truth I'd fall a martyr,
>> Truth from lips that will not lie.
>
> Give to me thine inspiration,
>> Let thy soul my soul immerse
> Till through sweetest meditation
>> I can sing my soul in verse.

Reed's post-graduation walking trips through England, France and Spain reinforced this dominance of the old world.

In New York the opposing tugs of romance and reality first became apparent. Pulling one way were the successful men who elected him to their Dutch Treat Club, Mabel Dodge and her sensuality and disdain of the world, the bohemianism which enveloped Reed in Greenwich Village; in the other direction, despite his opposite intentions, pulled Lincoln Steffens, the Paterson labor leaders Arthur Giovannitti, Carlo Tresca and Elizabeth Gurley Flynn, the very city itself. Day and night he studied New York, anatomy and physiology, watched the skyscrapers thrust up from its bowels, became part of the herds pouring from its sweatshops, wandered around the East Side, stood on dark corners near Union Square to watch the city's midnight.

To one who has himself fallen under the enchantment of the metropolis, Reed's poems and sketches of New York reach into its viscera to grasp at the heart. But passion for this gorgeous monstrosity can mean many things. It is one thing to replace mediaeval castles with skyscrapers; it is another to see below its surfaces into the lives of its creators. It was not until two years before his death, in "America, 1918," that Reed expressed in verse his mature love of New York. At the beginning it is only a partial substitute for the realm of Arthur. The images in which he describes the "foundations of a skyscraper" are left-overs of mediaevalism: the spotlight which makes night-work possible produces beams "sharp as a sword"; the excavation is "like dragons' lairs"; the skyscraper itself is "a phantom of fair towers." Whatever elements in the city pushed Reed toward the left are not to be found in the short poems written there.

For the essential problem facing Reed in New York at this time was bohemianism. Hindsight demonstrates that bohemianism, with its emphasis on idiosyncrasy for its own sake and its violent opposition to discipline, was an obstacle in Reed's development toward the revolutionary. Evidence for the conquest of this obstacle should be sought in Reed's action rather than in his poetry, and will be found sufficiently in his support of Max Eastman's demand for a *Masses* with a political program and in the many days and nights he devoted to the cause of the silk-strikers in Paterson. But the struggle with bohemianism also received expression in Reed's poetry and nowhere better than in his longest and best work, *The Day in Bohemia.*

This description of a day in Greenwich Village is properly traced back to the poems written for *Lampoon.* It shows the humor of college days flowered into satire, and exhibits his rebelliousness before the early grim stage of revolution, which Reed did not live to overcome, had pressed smiles from his lips and laughter from his thoughts.

Number Forty-Two still stands facing the south side of Washington Square park, surrounded by a Greenwich Village, despite the advent of tourists, advertising and high rents, the center for the "great souls of our little time" whom Reed found there, the

> Inglorious Miltons by the score,—
> Mute Wagners,—Rembrandts, ten or more,—
> And Rodins, one to every floor.

The same "characters"—although probably in fewer number—wander around the fountain, and there exist most of the same restaurants and hotels, although now much more expensive and exclusive.

Reed lived dowstairs at 42 with three Harvard cronies, under the very tolerant surveillance of Lincoln Steffens in the upper story. He was at that time an up-and-coming young journalist and verse-writer, on the staff of *The American Magazine,* and associating with successful men of letters and the arts as a member of the Dutch Treat Club. The poem, with many digressions in the form of incidental songs, describes a day in Reed's life from early morning till late night. Beginning with a description of the Village, enumeration of its celebrities, restaurants and alleys, and a tongue-in-cheek exaltation of bohemian life, Reed brings us to Number 42 on a Tuesday morning to watch the antics of four healthy young men waking and preparing for the day. He himself arrives quite late at the office of *The American Magazine* and soon goes out to the weekly luncheon of the Dutch Treat Club, taking this opportunity to praise the Club and to name its more prominent members.

In the afternoon, rejection of Reed's poem, "The Minstrel of Romance," leads to a jumbled debate on the art of poetry in which Matthew Arnold is opposed against Walt Whitman and from which Reed escapes as it begins "raging o'er a phrase of Aristotle." He goes to an "aesthetic tea" in the studio of "Umbilicus" and there meets and satirically describes the characters of Village bohemianism. At home again, the four roommates are joined by friends and all make off to supper at Paglieri's restaurant on 11th Street. After supper, the landlady comes to ask for rent and is pacified amid much horseplay with $10 borrowed from Bob Hallowell. Others arrive, including Walter Lippmann and Alan Seeger, and there are hot discussions of politics, art and humanity. Reed, Seeger and two friends go out for a late snack at the Lafayette and return to fall asleep while one roommate types copy for the morrow and a visitor talks on and on about his borrowed philosophy.

The central core of the satire, in which Reed expressed his disgust with the Village's extreme bohemianism, is the description of the "aesthetic tea" at the studio of Umbilicus. Umbilicus had so much travelled round the world imitating better painters than himself and playing the roles of successive schools of art, and

At last he knew so much, he was so deft,
That neither vision, fire, nor self was left.

He became an instuctor at the Art Students' League, teaching that
"Art is not Art that cannot published be." His studio, airless, dusky,
its "Artistic Atmosphere" preserved with Chinese punk and scented
candles, is filled with paintings which remain unfinished because to
do so would be to compete with nature, who herself "is never quite
complete."

The tea is attended by representatives of all forms of bohe-
mianism: Bufo, the "Art-for-Art's-sake out-and-outer" who pro-
duces one short verse a year; Shaemus, "who out-revives the Celt
revival"; long-haired Trimalchio, who wants artists "steeped in all
the vices"; Strephon, the nature poet who never leaves his steam-
heated flat; Chloe, whose "job in life is simply to inspire"; Lilith, the
local sensualist; the Rich Man who plays at patron of the arts;
Flascus, the drunkard; Sporus, the anarchist who "wouldn't feel
quite safe without police"; Balbus, "a socialist from nose to chin";
Bubo, who thinks "painters should exist in dirt." Lumping them all
together, Reed attacks their dilettantism, their avant-garde pet-
tiness, their selfishness, their fantastic arguments in favor of
fashionable "wild theories" discarded by better thinkers, their ab-
sorption with sex, their squabbles "o'er some puling poet's
line"—all these disgust Reed. In the midst of the recitation of "A
Sonnet in A-Flat" by "Hafiz, the Prince of Syrio-Persian Larks," he
grabs his hat and flees. His anger and aversion are well expressed in
"Hynm to Manhattan":

O let some young Timotheus sweep his lyre
Hymning New York. Lo! Every tower and spire
Puts on immortal fire.
This city, which ye scorn
For her rude sprawling limbs, her strength unshorn—
Hands blunt from grasping, Titan-like, at Heaven,
Is a world-wonder, vaulting all the Seven!
Europe? Here's all of Europe in one place;
Beauty unconscious, yes, and even grace.
Rome? Here all that Rome was, and is not;
Here Babylon—and Babylon's forgot.
Golden Byzantium, drunk with pride and sin,

Carthage, that flickered out where we begin...
London? A swill of mud in Shakespeare's time;
Ten Troys lie tombed in centuries of grime!
Who'd not have lived in Athens at her prime,
Or helped to raise the mighty walls of Rome?
See, blind men! Walls rise all about you here at home!
Who would not hear once more
That oceanic roar
"Ave! Ave Imperator!"
With which an army its Augustus greets?
Hark! There's an army roaring in the streets!
This spawning filth, these monuments uncouth,
Are but her wild, ungovernable youth.
But the skyscrapers, dwarfing earthly things—
Ah, that is how she sings!
Wake to the vision shining in the sun;
Earth's ancient, conquering races rolled in one,
A World beginning—*and yet nothing done!*

This romantic expression of the soul of New York which he urged
upon other poets, Reed himself postponed for five years. But within
these years he changed. He not only discarded bohemianism, but
also the worship of the European past; he momentarily moved in his
verse from romanticism to naturalism—in short, he became a
radical.

Reed wrote fewer than a score of original poems after *The Day in
Bohemia*. Shortly after its publication, he identified himself with the
striking silk workers of Paterson and on June 7, 1913, staged the
Pageant of the Paterson strike in Madison Square Garden. At the
same time he met and became the lover of Mabel Dodge, a wealthy
woman of the world who had established a salon a few blocks from
Washington Square. Perhaps inflamed by love of her, perhaps
wearied by the labor of staging the Pageant, perhaps running away
from the responsibilities of association with anarchist labor leaders,
Reed sailed for Europe with Mabel Dodge within a week after the
Pageant.

That this short stay in Italy was a period of crisis for John Reed
can be seen in the single poem remaining from it and unknown until
published by Mabel Dodge Luhan in 1936. Reading it and looking

back to the period which produced it with the eye of a woman for whom the "ultimate sexual act" is "the cornerstone of any life and its chief reality," Mrs. Luhan finds in it a resolution of the conflict between herself and the world for control of Reed's affections. "I hated to see him interested in Things," she writes

> I wasn't and didn't like to have him even *look* at churches and leave me out of his attentions... I had more than stones to make me jealous. Reed was terribly interested in *people*. I lost him every hour to humans...And when finally he capitulated to me and agreed that the past was past and the old age of Italian wonder was wearisome, he wrote this poem; and that day I knew I need not fear Italy any more.

It is strange that a man expressing his love for a woman should write: "In her right hand a man's death; in her left the life of a man." In a sense, Reed did choose Mabel: he chose her left hand and went back to New York with her. But her right hand still held "a man's death." When they quarreled shortly afterwards, he sent her the following note:

> Good-bye my darling. I cannot live with you. You smother me. You crush me. You want to kill my spirit. I love you better than life but I do not want to die in my spirit. I am going away to save myself. Forgive me. I love you. I love you.

When John Reed rejected the great Italian past he was not doing it for the body of Mabel Dodge but for the very "spirit" which she insisted on suppressing. How else can one interpret these lines?

> Here where the olden poets came in beauty to die
> I sit in a walled high garden, far from the sound
>   of change,
> Watching the great clouds boil up from the
>   Vallombrosa range
> And sunlight pour through the black cypresses,
>   drenching the vineyards dry.
> Here is the drunken peace of the sensuous sick,—
>   and here am I,

Smelling the smoke from clanging cities, that
   hangs like a threat in the sky
Unknown to these clods
Who worship Bacchus and Pan, and the senile young gods!

For John Reed, the past as a source of romance was now largely dead, and that strain in him which demanded it had to be satisfied within the present.

Such satisfaction he found as a correspondent in Mexico sharing with Villa's soldiers the fundamental joys and dangers felt so deeply by men, however ignorant, who think they fight for a great ideal. But Mexico is not to be found in his poetry except in a handful of unpolished translations of ballads of local life, love and politics. Even the choice of these particular ballads cannot be considered as evidence reflecting Reed's development, for they may well have been the only ones known by his particular comrades-through-chance. But indeed, poetry is no longer Reed's major mode of expression. The few poems of his last seven years are mere glimpses through a window of his soul which is almost always closed, but behind which they are unified by the flow of his life.

Sitting with his back against one of the lichened walls of hand-placed stones that crisscross New England, he looks out at nature in its dreariest time, the moment between autumn and winter, before the snow has hidden the corpses of the vegetable world and before complete bareness against a field of white endows the trees with silhouettes of striking beauty.

So, gazing upon last year's furrows, and the marks
   of old ploughs,
And the drear scattered houses, feathered with
   little smoke,
And the lean cattle backing to the wind,
And the dun hobbling man stiffly carrying in wood,
And the pale thwarted faces of their women at the
   windows,—
I thought, this is death,—this is lassitude and
   sterility, unending,—
Rock and weeds and back-bowing work have stunted
   the soul of this place,

Faith has the world none, nor future save fruitless,
   monotonous drudgery,—
Stunted souls too weary to aspire,—and deadened
   brains too driven to do better.

Examination of Reed's last poems leaves no doublt that he intend-
ed to continue to create and made an attempt to fuse poetry with
radical politics in such proportion as to maintain poetic quality and
not to produce mere propaganda. He achieved a measure of success
in "Hospital Notes" and "Two Rooms"; in "Without That Ye Lifted
A Hand" he failed.

On November 22, 1916, John Reed's ailing left kidney, the cause
of much illness since childhood, was removed at Johns Hopkins
Hospital. From his stay in the wards two poems emerged. "Hospital
Notes," with naturalist precision expressed in closely budgeted free
verse, presents the institution as an impersonal machine, wholly and
in its parts oblivious to human suffering.

Square white cells, all in a row, with ground-glass
   windows;
Tubes treasuring sacraments of suffering, rubber pipes,
   apparatus;
Walls maculate with old yellow and brown....
Out of a mass of human flesh, hairy and dull,
Slim shining steel grows, dripping slow pale thick
   drops,
And regularly, like distant whistles in a fog,
   groaning....
Young interns, following the great surgeon like
   chicks a hen,
Crowd in as he pokes, wrenches, and dictates over
   his shoulders,
And hurries on, deaf to the shuddering spirit,
   rapt in a dream of machinery.

"Two Rooms" again presents this contrast between the human
patient and the machinelike hospital, between the sufferer and the
doctor who says

"It's our duty, you know,
To preserve life as long as possible—and besides,
The last stages are particularly interesting..."

But the poem goes beyond this to contrast the rich and the poor, in their life and in their death. Bertram C. Pick, the Ice Trust Millionaire, comes to an elaborate suite to die of Bright's Disease produced by dissipation. Two specialists care for him, hourly bulletins are given the anxious press, a private nurse is in constant attendance. Outside the death-room his daughter plans an immediate trip abroad to "have some fun."

Toward the end, as he twisted gasping on his bed
In that quiet room, with his special nurses, and
  orderlies,
And all that science can do, to ease his body,
And orchids to ease his soul, and telegrams and
  cables from kings, presidents, parliaments,
  stock-exchanges—
I wondered if his burning kidney reminded him
Of that hot summer, when the fevered slums
Spewed out dead babies, and he made his pile...

To a small room endowed by a magnate's widow comes a withered bricklayer, his body worn out with labor, dying of an infected urinary system which "A year's rest in a warm climate" might have cleared up. His wife comes to pay in advance for five weeks and then goes home to earn whatever else will be due. Ill-treated by the attendants who withhold the pain-relieving morphine until his screams wake up the whole ward, he dies suffering.

Well, he stayed in 53—so his wife was working.
And before the dope stopped acting, he was so weak
You could hardly hear his wheezing moan at all,
Although you knew his soul was screaming always....
And then even that stopped, and the nurse sighed
Relievedly....
But all I could think of was death in 53
Without love, or battle, or any glorious suddenness...

A poet who can thus infuse his art with love of mankind need not worry about the charge of propaganda. But greater difficulty—and in Reed's case failure—attends the attempt to carry poetry with direct political slogans. The fragment here titled, for convenience, "Without That Ye Lifted A Hand," was never completed. It is my own opinion that this was intentional, that Reed's sense of poetry could not be satisfied with lines like these:

> Without that ye lifted a hand, without that ye
> uttered a cry,
> While ye stood there stupidly wondering, as the
> ox stands to die,
> All ye had won in a thousand years the Masters
> took again,
> And drove your sons to be butchered, and butcher
> the German men.

Reed's love of mankind received further expression in what is almost his last poem, "America, 1918." Marred by too superficial an imitation of Whitman and by a lack of mastery of free-verse form, the poem nevertheless succeeds in expressing Reed's love of New York as seen in his memories of it while in Europe. It is the deep love of a man pained by the moral separation between himself and his homeland, by his own feeling that he is alien to it. Attempting to recapture his America

> ....my lost one, my first lover
> I love no more, love no more, love no more...

he goes over the experiences of his life as they led him across her body from the far Northwest to Harvard and then to New York. Describing, cataloguing, he stretches out his arms to reach for this world. Perhaps its best section is the description of Greenwich Village.

> Old Greenwich Village, citadel of amateurs,
> Battle-ground of all adolescent Utopias,
> Half sham-Bohemia, dear to uptown slummers,
> Half sanctuary of the outcast and dissatisfied...
> Free fellowship of painters, sailors, poets,

Light women, Uranians, tramps, and strike-leaders,
Actresses, models, people with aliases or nameless,
Sculptors who run elevators for a living,
Musicians who pound pianos in picture-houses...
Workers, dissipating, most of them young, most
    of them poor,
Playing at art, playing at love, playing at rebellion,
In the enchanted borders of the impossible republic...

Mysteriously has word of it gone forth
To lonely cabins in the Virginia mountains,
Logging-camps in the Maine woods, desert ranches,
Farms lost in vastnesses of Dakota wheat...
Wherever young heart-hungry dreamers of splendor
Can find in all the hard immensity of America
No place to fashion beauty, no companion
To shameless talk of loveliness and love,
Here would they be, elbow on a wooden table at
    Polly's,
Or, borrowing a fiver, over Burgundy at the Brevoort,
Arguing about Life, and Sex, and the Revolution...

This was the John Reed whom Thomas Beer met one day on River-
side Drive and who began to talk about the America he knew, "and
was not a playboy about it....He said nothing profound, but he
made beauty, talking. Men do that when they have talked about
things they have loved much."

John Reed's last poem was written to his wife, Louise Bryant. It is
perhaps unjust, considering the circumstances of its composition, to
seek in it a reflection of the tendencies of his life, of the opposing
movements within it between romance and reality, but its position at
the end of his days is perhaps important as a symbol. "Two Rooms,"
"Hospital Notes," "America, 1918," point to a Reed who as a poet
might at last have successfully fused his art with love of the common
people and radical political philosophy; but "A Letter to Louise,"
recalling the products of a romanticism not yet entirely obliterated
within him, may give us just the hint of a doubt.

Perhaps the Reed who was a Communist would have gone on with
that party through all its difficulties and vacillations and metamor-

phoses and been its staunch adherent today; but certain actions on the eve of his death also give us just the hint of a doubt and have indeed resulted in a fight for the possession of John Reed between opposing factions of the left. Just as the future of his politics was uncertain, so also was the future of his poetry. What remains today in these pages is a miscellaneous collection, unified in their reflection of the torques of reality and romance as they fought across his soul, and constituting a twisted arrow whose final direction it is forever impossible to determine.

Leo Stoller
June, 1947

COLLECTED POEMS

The Chicken

(With apologies to the shade of Poe)

I

Once upon a midnight dreary as I chuckled weak and weary
Over many a saintly "Spinster" and unsaintly "Troubadour"
While I chortled nearly splitting, suddenly there came hitting
As of someone gently kicking, biffing at my chamber door,
Only that and nothing more.

II

And the rustling of the stitches on my Sunday pair of
    britches
Thrilled me—filled me with fantastic terrors never felt
    before.
So my faint heart to be quelling, I stood while loudly
    yelling
"Hurry up, come in, you idiots, and be sure to close the
    door"
Silence there, and nothing more.

III

Presently my wrath grew stronger; hesitating then no longer,
I walked over to the threshold and threw wide my chamber door
Deep into the darkness peering, long I stood there, wondering,
    fearing,
Fearing muchly to be smitten with a rotten apple core,
Merely this and nothing more.

IV

Back into my chamber turning, all my heart with wrath aburning
Soon again I heard the biffing, somewhat louder than before.

3

"Surely" said I "surely that is eggs against my window-lattice
For it soundeth like the shoes of Brother Mike upon the floor.
That it is and nothing more."

V

Open wide I flung the shutter, when, with many a flirt and
      flutter,
In there stepped a stately chicken of the saintly days of
      yore
Not the least obeisance made she; not an instant stopped
    or stayed she
Perching on the bust of Bill Nye just above my chamber door,
Laid an egg upon the floor.

VI

Then methought the air grew denser, perfused from
      an unseen censor
Swung by editors whose footsteps tinkled in the
      corridor.
"Wretch" I cried "A spirit lent thee—but to haunt
    me here he sent thee.
Get thee hence, and never darken with thy wing my
      chamber door!"
Quoth the chicken "Nevermore"

VII

"Prophet" said I "Thing of evil!—prophet still,
    if hen or devil,
Tell me, will P. Herriott ever get a readmittance more?
Will Fourteenth Street gate be cut through, and the
    happy children butt through?
And won't they have to go around the long way as
    before?"
Crowed the chicken, "Nevermore!"

VIII

"Be that word our sign of parting, bird or fiend,"

4

I shrieked, upstarting
"Take thy feet from off my Bill Nye and the eggs
        from off my door!"
But the chicken never flitting, on my Bill Nye still
        is sitting,
And the egg that lies within the shadow floating
        on the floor
Shall be lifted—*nevermore!*

Origo

This—with the sigh of the dark sad trees that stand
Aloft on yon battlement, looking across the land
Rooted age-deep in the crumbling canyon rock
Suffering, fog-wreathed, the sea-driven tempest's shock
This—where the gloomy walls of the river's bed
Climb toward the forest murmuring overhead,
Yearning the song of the soft Chinook that bears
Smiles for the fruitful lands, for the arid, tears;
With the luminous moon so soft behind the mist
And a thin sweet star that a spruce's tuft has kissed.

I seem the first to have seen this, I the last
I the only one, yet in ages past
Who knows but some Indian, treading at dusk the wood,
Paused on the edge of the bluff, and listening, stood
Then just as I, with a shower of crumbling clay
Half climbed, half slipped to the bottom where twilight gray
Already was veiling the wondrous face of Day.
Long time he stood and the roar of the upper fall
Beat in his ears. From the top of the canyon wall
A black hawk lifted, and sailing across the sky
Portended evil, harshly sounding his cry.
Then gazing about him, waded the icy stream
Where the dim cliffs like misty phantoms seem
Ghosts from the realm of some forgotten dream.

And as the demon darkness swallowed the light
Donning his starry armor, diamond-bright
The firelight touched the Indian's swarthy face
As he crooned some song of his mystic, savage race.
And the moon peeped down from the feathered cloud she rode
Where a silver stream through a silver canyon flowed.

Then, Dawn was born and with the coming light
The Eagle Sun soared from the realm of night
Then roused himself the Indian, sprang far out
Into a shadowed pool and threshed about
With tawny limbs. Emerged with body bare
And shook the water from his shining hair
Then, dripping crystal drops, he climbed the wall
And standing like a gleaming statue tall
Against the forest green he gazed once more
Down where the living water chafed its shore
The silver trout that leaped from out the stream
And the murmur like the whisper of a dream
Long-past and half-forgotten, soft and sweet
The patter of innumerable feet
Adown the twilight of Eternity.
He turned, and soundless, vanished.

The Storm at Midnight

'Tis midnight; on the high and barren cliff
I stand and watch the ragged, sombre clouds,
Driven by the furious gale across the moon,
Make shadows on the ocean's heaving breast.
Below me, beating on the rocky coast,
The gleaming breakers crash; and on the beach
The booming surf falls sullenly. Its spray,
Hurled up and onward by the hurricane,
Stings bitter on my face, and leaves behind
The breath of ocean ling'ring in the air.

Far out to sea, a vessel on her course
Buffets the storm. I see her heaving lights
Rise on the wave and plunge into the trough,
Scudding bare-poled into the dusky night.
The thunder mutters angrily, and low
The lightning-bolts, Zeus driven, cleave the sky
And hurtle into darkness.
An atom in this world of might and night,
I stand alone.

Thermopylae

As I stand upon the mountain
Gazing down into the shadows
Of the grave of Leonidas,
Once again the sea is beating
Restlessly against the boulders;
Once again the mighty army
of the Persians, rolling onward,
Scourged to battle by its masters,
With a roaring like the ocean
Breaks upon the iron Spartans,
Like the surf upon the sea-shore,
And like it, is tumbled backward,
Whipped and cowed, its spirit broken,
Gashed and torn and sorely wounded.
Once again brave Leonidas,
Aided by the flower of Sparta,
Raising loud the inspiring pasan,
Holds at bay ten thousand Persians.
Shock on shock of bloody battle
Mingled with the savage war-song,
Raise the symphony of Ares
To the silent hills behind them.
Suddenly the Spartans wheeling

Find the enemy behind them,
And between two rows of murder,
One by one face death unflinching,
While the setting sun glows redly
On the bodies of dead heroes.

But no more the great sea surges
Restlessly against the cliff-side,
And no more the mad fight rages
Making red the sea beneath it.
But upon the scene descendeth
As the sun sinks slowly seaward,
Hallowed calm which seems to bless those,
Who thus died to save their country.

Lost

(A Sonnet)

I

King Arthur passed away into the night.
Borne upon his sombre barge along,
While through the dark there thrilled a wondrous song
To Bedevere gazing with tear-dimmed sight.
Straight to the east into the ashy light
Of dawn, the strange ship held its lonely way,
And like a sunbeam, in the eye of day
The king's helm flashed far out upon the bight.
The old, true days are gone; the future lies
As dark and cheerless as the morning grey.
The dreary country-side before his eyes
Wakes a dull pain, as on his weary way
The knight returns. A brooding vulture flies
Toward the fateful field of yesterday.

II

Danais passed away into the night
Of my black thoughts; by angels borne along,
And going, seemed to breathe a wondrous song
To me who stood and gazed with tear-dimmed sight.
Straight to the east into the holy light
Of love for Him, she held her happy way,
And like a sunbeam in the eye of day
Her farewell flashed to me across the bight.
The old true days are gone, the future lies
As dark and cheerless as the morning grey.
A dreary life before my saddened eyes
Unfolds, as wearily I go my way
While in my heart, from out the darkness rise
The happy memories of yesterday.

Our Lady of Pain

Brown waffles and mellow molasses
Welsh rarebit that bites us and burns
Budweiser that fills up our glasses
The waiter that turns and returns
When these have gone by with their glories
What then to our stomachs remain?
Thou! Mystic and savage Dolores
Our Lady of Pain!

We physic and doctor and dope us
Thou art smoking and tempting and hot
What matter if pains telescope us
We eat thee, dyspepsia or not.
Nor health nor hygiene is the question
So fill up the bumpers again
Thou wilt come when we have indigestion
Our Lady of Pain

"Jolly Boating Weather"

I

Who are those skeletons ill-clad a-splashing
    on the river
And other naked spectres who stand round the
    float and shiver?
Are they those Cambridge muckers that go swim-
    ming from the bank,
Or are they ghosts of former "mucks" with chains
    that clash and clank?
Ah, no, although they may not yet be oarsmen
    through and through,
Still they are members of a famous dormitory crew.

II

What is it makes the noble brow, and makes the
    chest swell out,
Or causes men, as you pass by, to volunteer a
    shout?
Is it because perhaps you may have saved a baby's
    life,
Or stabbed William Randolph in the stomach with
    a knife?
Nay, you will choose a nobler deed when noble
    deeds you do,
You'll say, "I am the man that made his dormitory
    crew! Did you?"

Pan

Where the lone loon, deep in the shadow of the
    gloomy pines,
Sends through the dark his tragic laugh across
    some Northern lake,

Thrilling the dusk, a sad refrain inexplicably
　　sweet,
There let me life, care-free, to Paradise un-
　　dreamed awake.

What if, at dawn, I hear among the trees a
　　dreary note—
The wood-god's pipe, forever mourning in its
　　lonely song
The gods of old, who died in anguish on the
　　Cross with Christ,—
Where Pan, deep-hidden, dreams again that he
　　is young.

Forgotten Pan, no more impassioned Nymphs
　　dance on the hill
Beneath the moon, with thee to sway the
　　measure of their dance,
In far-off Greece, but here, deep in the
　　silent, ancient wood,
Pipe out thy soul, and trembling, hide from
　　God at day's advance.

The Tempest

As Pallas sprang from the head of Zeus,
　　Divine in her splendid mail,
I leapt full-armed from the Sun-god's brow
　　And rode on the roaring gale.
A Thousand leagues to the east we fled,
　　While heaven and earth and sea
Arose to the tread of my mighty feet
　　In terrible symphony.
I sang of wars in the dawn of time,
　　Of worlds in the outer night,
I stabbed the dark with my two-edged sword,
　　And struck in a burst of light.
The great ship drove on the rocks aflame,

A towering funeral pyre,
While I swooped down on the shattered coast
And tortured the land with fire.

. . . .

But lo! the heart of the mystic cast
Is drawling the veil away,
I weaken, bound in a drowsy charm,
The spell of another day.
My father comes; with a slower pace,
I languidly seek my rest.
And deep in the poppied warmth I sink
Asleep on the Sun-god's breast.

California

These many years the hoary missions lie
Under the turquoise sky
Smiling, like white-haired priests asleep,
Who dream of happy memories.
And still the blue Sierras keep
Their ancient guard above the flow'ring orange trees.
When softly, like a dusky cowl,
The odorous night wraps round the day,
And in the purple deep
The dying sun is laid away,
His only requiem a mournful owl,
Alone, and owl-like, mourning unremembered wrong.
Then rings the ghostly Angelus so sweet
That, shattered by a song,
The years turn back to Spanish nights
Two hundred years ago; and from the street
The mellow twang of the guitar
Some dark-eyed belle invites
Out into the star-gardens of the sky
And passes in the distance down the road
From Santa Barbara to Mirimar.

12

Harvard—Yale, 1950

The Harvard airship Hockey Team had trained for
    many a day,
They passed the puck with the best of luck in
    many a crafty way;
And the papers said that old Yale was dead and
    that Harvard had 'em cold,
With the same old wail of a hard luck tale, as
    it was in the days of old.

At the signal gun was the game begun, and two of
    mighty girth
Faced off on high in the midst of the sky and shot
    for the ends of earth.
There was blood that day on the Milky Way 'mid the
    flying puck's shrill scream,
And the Cherubim left off their hymn to bet on
    the Eli team.

One broke his stick by an awful lick, but the
    grand stand went insane
When a spike he tore from the roof of Gore and
    swatted the puck again
With wings unfurled they skimmed the world and
    battled around the Bear,
But Hugh McGuff of Yale was rough, and they
    ruled him off the air.

No score was made, but our forwards played with
    the strength of a hundred men,
Till we shot a goal from the far North Pole which
    won us the game again.
And with cheer and song the whole night long we
    evened up ancient debts,
But the cherubs sold their crowns of gold to pay
    off their losing bets.

13

The Desert

This solemn waste is hushed forevermore,
And nothing lives, but on the shifting sand
Lost souls trace with imponderable hand
The hieroglyphics of their mystic lore.
Like ruins of some old, Titanic war
The shattered desert lies; nor wakes the land
Save to the thunder's furious saraband,
When armored lightning smites the rocky floor.
All night the caravans of stars go by
In silence. Still the sombre wasteland keeps
Its lonely watch while all high heaven sleeps,
And the lone moon is drowsy in the sky. . . .

How delicate the trembling thrill that leaps
From heart to heart as the pale star-fires die!

Medical School Song

Give a rouse then for the clinic
And the genial autopsy,
For we're everyone a cynic
With a medical degree.
For it's always fair weather
When medicos get together,
With a spine on the table
And a lancet swinging free.

Oh, we get 'em at all ages,
From the cradle to the tomb,

And our laughter is contagious
In the operating-room.
For it's always fair weather
When medicos get together,
With a spine on the table
And a lancet swinging free.

The Pacific

Sunset.

Gulls to their home on the aged rock,
Wheeling athwart the spray,
Thrill of the wind from the Isles of Ind.
In the heart of the dying day.

I

Out of the wrack of the tortured sky
Out of the hymn of the stars
I made you a song from the chants of old
And the clamor of ancient wars

II

Heavy and slow
Restlessly, hopelessly yearning to me.
Is there no peace in the breast of the ocean.
Is there no sleep on the eyes of the sea?
Softly and low
Mourning forever the gods of the sea
Swaying forever in tremulous motion
Stretching its wet little wave-hands to me.

15

The West

Gulls to their home on the aged rock
    Wheeling athwart the spray,
Thrill of the wind from the isles of Ind
    In the heart of the dying day.

Dreams in the depths of the solemn pines
    Ancient before our birth,
Hearing the speech of the plains that reach
    To the ends of the happy earth.

Out of the years that have passed away
    Out of the days to be,
Night brings the pang of the salt air's tang
    And the call of the West to me

Coyote Song

A-oo, my brothers, the moon is red,
And the antelope starts from his prairie bed—
Then join ye again in the ancient threne
For the day that's dead,
And the hunt that's fled,
And the terror of things unseen!

Afar, afar on the starlit plain
Our fathers howled where the door had lain,
And hung on the flanks of the bison run—
For the bull that fell
In the wild pell-mell
Had died ere the night was done!

No more the warrior rides his raids,
And the hunting-star of the prairie fades;

While a fiery comet tears the night,
With a crimson streak—
And a demon shriek—
All ablaze with the white man's light!

But oft when the winter winds are high,
We hear on the prairie the bellowed cry
And the rumbling hoofs on the bison run—
But we seek in vain
Through the empty plain,
For the buffalo days are done. . . .

A-oo, my brothers! The stars are red,
And the lean coyote must mourn unfed.
Come join ye again in the ancient croon—
For the dawn is grey
And another day
Has faded the red, red moon.

The Sea Gull

Wet with the stinging spray he skims the deep,
A livid gleam of life, and scans afar
Where the great breakers pound across the bar,
Beneath the headlands where his nestlings sleep.
Above the light the keeper sees him sweep
From fog to fog, and vanish like a star
Down where the unknown ocean monsters are,
And hears his mournful crying on the steep.

And when on winter days he rises high
Against the squall, and swift on-coming night,
And bares his gleaming armor to the fight,
Then are the sailors startled by his cry;
Darting spear-like athwart the dark'ning main
To ride the helmet of the hurricane.

Ideas

I

Where the old volumes, weltering in Gore,
Lie 'mid a heap of *Crimsons* on the floor,
There do we turn for new ideas once more.

II

Once more the ever-verdant "fresh" is here,
Once more he sips audacious drafts of beer,
Once more we search the files of yester year.

III

Here is the yearly *"Crimesown* Candidate,"
"Letters to Paw" and "Jonathan's First Skate,"
"First Cigarette" too awful to relate.

IV

Old whispered quips of Mom. and agile choose,
"And your exams? I passed them all with E's,"
What would we do without a host of these?

The Seventh Ode of the Fourth Book of Horace

All fled are the snows; now
the meadows and forests awaken
Clothed in their beautiful hair
The land thrills anew with
the change and the rivers subsiding
Flow with a languider air.

Again in the moonlight
the grace intertwined with her sisters
    Sways in the passionate dance
    "Hope not for Eternity" saying,
The Year and the Moment
    Hasten the bright day's advance.

All night the swift moons
in the heavens renew their lost brilliance
    Yet when we go to our doom
    Where Tullius has gone, and
Aeneas our father, and Ancus
    We are but dust of the tomb.

Who knows if the high gods
will crown with another tomorrow
    This summer sky of today?
    Be happy then, living, for
riches, once you have departed,
    Heirs will but lavish away.

When once you have fallen,
Torquatus, and over your spirit
    Minos has given decree
    Then not all your goodness,
nor treasurer, nor silver-tongued pleading
    Ever can bring you to me.

For neither can Artesis
free from the terrible darkness
    Pure-hearted Hippolytus
    Now can the strong Theseus unloose
the dread chains that imprison
    Thrice-loved Pirithros.

Score

No hope for Eli
Here's where we score
Come twist the bull-dog's tail,
We'll win once more,
For Harvard's back at New Haven,
Hark to their mournful wail!
It might be worse,
Boys, call up a hearse
For poor old Yale.

A Winter Run

Out of the warmth and light,
    Into the frosty weather,
Into the teeth of a winter's night,
    Running, we sprang together.

The icy, silent dark leapt up
    And struck me in the face—
And the moon hung out her silver cup
    As trophy for the race.

Our driving breath flung out behind
    Like some dim, flying plume;
Our shadows, on the snow outlined,
    Ran with us in the gloom.

The long white road, the rhythmic beat,
    The wind-sword in our hair—
Oh, here's the spell of winged feet,
    The charm of winter air!

A flashing glimpse, a scarce-seen face,
    A figure clear, then gone,

Once more the dark, the swinging pace,
    And on again, and on.

Across the river dim and still
    The headless sleepers lie,
And, finger-like, the towered hill
    Stands up against the sky.

Into the warmth and the light,
    Out of the frosty weather,
Out of the chill of a winter's night,
    Glowing, we sprang together.

And Yet—

Here do we part, you and the rest to stay
    In the red valley where the lotus weaves
Glad pain with sleep; and up the rugged way
    I go alone, and wish I might forget.
    And yet—and yet—

The sun is on the upland sheaves,
And all the grass with starry tears is wet.

Work! Work! Something to dull the ache
    Of petty friends and little souls—ah, vain,
All vain the grief that you and you awake.
    Gone is the old unutterable thrill,
    And still—and still—

I hear from out the driving wraiths of rain
The brown thrush singing on the upland hill.

Sternes

Primeval Sternes, upon whose massive frame
Great strength has set its everlasting mark,
Each day our envious respect you claim
As up the Charles you stroke your graceful bark.

The wicked dread you and the good revere
Stern guard of Harvard's morals, you alone
The wild inebriate regards with fear
You lend us our aristocratic tone

While strains of "Dearie" wafted to our ears
Moves some to ribald laughter, some to tears
Remember Sampson shorn and take good care
To keep a watchful eye upon your hair

Roosevelt

A mollycoddle is not a man
And never a man he'll be
Till Eli wins from Harvard's crew
Another victory

This face benign, this figure fine
Are found in every publication
Some laud him to the firmament
Some show a keen disapprobation.

Writer, fighter, peace-inviter
Brave and fiery speech-reciter
Arbitrator, legislator,
Up-to-date caluminator
Early riser, like the Kaiser
Nature's Revolutioniser
May they all be true and ready
Like our Uncle Sammy's Teddy

Then come what may, be this your stay
Forever in eternity
Though all be lost, yet you are still
A veritas celebrity

Forgetfulness

Adapted from the French of Heredia

The temple falls to ruin on the cape,
And utter sleep has mingled with the mold
The marble gods and paladine of old,—
Locked in the prison whence is no escape.
Sometimes the lonely herdsman drives his kine
To the clear lake, and wakes the ancient pain,
With the sad piping of an old refrain,
Clear-cut against the far horizon-line;
The kindly earth guards well its old regime,
And each Spring, vainly eloquent, doth dower
The broken pillar with a new-born flower:
But man, unheedful of his father's dream,
Fears not to hear each night, unchangingly,
The vast, eternal sorrow of the sea

The Traveler

Adapted from the French of Heredia

He sailed from Egypt under pleasant skies,
Proud of his ship, and gazing toward the South,
Where Pharos faded at the harbour-mouth;
Nor did he heed Arcturus on the rise.
No more he'll see the Alexandrine mole—
But in the barren sand of some far shore,

Where one lone tree is wind-tossed evermore,
The storm has carved a chamber for his soul.

Laid in the deepest hollow of the dune,
The Traveler has found his rest at last,
Forever wrapped in starless, breathless night—
So still he lies beneath the Grecian moon.
Above his body, whence the fire has passed,
O Sea be silent, and O Earth be light!

The Slave

Adapted from the French of Heredia

Thus, naked, frightful, gaunt without food,
A Slave,—my body still retains the scares,—
I was born free, where, rising toward the stars,
Old honeyed Hybla lifts his mountain hood.
Alas, I left the happy isle; O friend,
If ever, following the swans' Spring flight,
Your galley's course toward Syracuse shall tend,
Seek her who was my love and my delight.
Is it ordained that I shall ever see
Her somber violet eyes, her heavenly smile,
Caught from the sky when all the gods were young?
Be merciful. Go! seek Cleariste for me,
And tell her to await me yet a while—
Know her you will, for she is always sad.

The Seven Ages

If all the world's a stage
Then all these Freshmen are but supers in it,
Thrust from the wings upon a brilliant scene

In seven divers costumes. First the Infant,
Mewling and puking at an Adviser's word,
Then the dumb timid Cub that sips his mug
At melancholy beer-nights. Then the Sport,
Friend of the chorus girl, whose idea of Heaven
Is the Touraine. And then the football hero,
Full of strange oaths and armoured like a knight,
Seeking the bubble Reputation
Even on the gridiron. Then the sober grind,
With eyes severe and water-wagon mien,
Slave to Probation. The sixth age shifts
Into a pale and qualmy Pantaloon,
New pipe in hand, tobacco pouch on side,
The privilege he coveted, too strong
For his unshaven lip; his breath comes quick
And whistles in his sound. Last scene of all,
Shorn of his soul, a would-be Sophomore
In second childishness and mere oblivion—
Sans wisdom, taste, sans thirst, sans—everything.

The Charge of the Political Brigade

Twenty votes, thirty votes,
Forty votes onward
Into the voting booth
Strode the three hundred.
"Forward the Fools' Brigade,
After their votes!" he said
So to the ballot box
Strode the three hundred.

"Forward, O Democrats!
Down with black Derby hats!"
How could the Party know
Someone had blundered?
Their's not to make reply,

Their's not to reason why,
Their's but to vote—and lie.
Into the voting booth
Strode the three hundred.

Pickets the right of them,
Jobs to the left of them,
Soreheads in front of them
Shouted and thundered.
Hounded with shot and shell
"Let the Street go to Hell
We'll do the job as well!"
As they collected votes,
Cried the three hundred.

"Charge the Committee then!"
Three hundred stalwart men,
Traitors to Nineteen Ten
Broke the class spirit while
All the world wondered.
Swayed by false argument,
Urged to the Polls they went,
Scoundrels and ignorant,
Worthy three hundred.

Mediaeval Gastronomy

I

'Tis not for such as I to doubt
Those mediaeval tales,
Yet oft they reach a point where the
Imagination fails.
The knights are dust, their good swords rust
The sad-eyed poet sings;
Yet, How *could* they wear such heavy clothes
And eat such heavy things?

26

II

Sir Brian de Bois Guilbert, in
His iron, B.V.D.'s,
Reclines at his ancestral board
Breakfasting at his ease.
A haunch of venison, two steaks,
And half a dozen quail,
Then, He tops it off with buckwheat cakes and
Thirteen mugs of ale.

III

Mon dieu, you'd think that after that
This gastronomic knight
Would be unwell for quite a spell,
Or leastways *hors de* fight.
But with an energy undimmed
He girds his trusty blade
And, Disdainfull of dyspepsia,
He starts a small Crusade.

IV

Squire Bacon, country gentleman,
An honest man and blunt,
Deserts the pack to take a snack
Before the rabbit hunt.
Plum pudding, boars' heads, rum, and beer
The worthy squire surrounds,
Then, Upon his horse,—'cross fields, of course,—
Pursues the yelling hounds.

V

Monsieur the Vicomte Roland at
The forefront of the battle
Devours veal pasty with one hand
And slays the Moors like cattle.
It seems to me a silly thing
That Roland was so hasty

27

When, He might have slain the infidels
   By feeding them the pasty.

VI

There are a score of proofs and more
   That those of other days
Surpassed the men of 1910
   In culinary ways
For Richielieu and Henry VIII
   Were partial to the pot,
And, Bold Robin Hood admired his food
   And ate an awful lot

VII

Those iron-stomached paladins
   Accomplished wondrous deeds,
Yet never did dyspepsia
   Bestow the widow's weeds.
They seemed at best just after lunch,
   When *we* seem half demented;
Now, I wonder if it was because
   One-thirties weren't invented?

Melisande

Ah, white, still sister of the blossom-fire,
your lips again! Across the twilight world
the driving wraiths of mist are hurled,
to shroud us in alone with our desire.

Torn by the silver talons of the rain
the wounded petals cover you,—less fair
than the wild fragrance of your hair,
less sweet than this sweet ecstasy of pain.

White maid, there is no God but the red flame
that burns so fiercely in your breast—no bliss
but the hot passion of your kiss—
no music but the whisper of your name.

One Way to Win

I

Ted Coogan was Yale's captain, a mighty man and bold,
He tipped the scale at thirty stone, was thirty-six
    years old,
Whene'er the fray was thickest—which was every
    little while—
You'd always find Ted Coogan at the bottom of the pile.

II

Now it came toward November, and with customary "sand,"
Ted rolled up scores by millions and won games on
    every hand,
And up to fourteen days before the yearly Harvard game
The bloody handed Elis had a sanguinary name.

III

Then swift about New Haven the sullen rumor ran,
"Our centre's got the measles, our tackle's off his can!"
Then from the Campus hurried Camp, his features blanched
    and pale,
And whispered, "Ted, what strategy can save the day for Yale?"

IV

Then shouted Ted, "Bright college years! By the nine
    gods of war!
The wearers of the Crimson H shall conquer Yale no more!
A plan!" he whispered in his ear, and grinning with
    delight,
With haste he pinned his first pin on, and vanished in
    the night.

V

Oh the Eli team was gloomy and the Eli throng was glum,
And the Eli coaches drowned their grief in quantities of rum;
But Camp remained undaunted, only arguing that he
("Since the game was up at Cambridge) should appoint a
    referee.

VI

The fatal day arrived at last, and out upon the field
The rival heroes trotted, and the rival bleachers reeled,
But no one knew the referee who stalked along the line,
His visage hid in whiskers and a frat pin on his spine.

VII

And suddenly the Elis shrieked aloud in wild despair,
For they looked to see their captain, and *Ted Coogan
    wasn't there!*
With the referee they pleaded to procrastinate the game,
But the referee was merciless and Harvard was the same.

VIII

I'll not tell how the whistle blew or how the
    heroes fought,
But in the second half, gadzooks! the score was
    naught to naught.
Then Harvard made a touchdown, and Yale went wild
    with fear.
When the referee stepped forth and cried, so all the
    world could hear,

IX

"The Crimson tackle held, egad!" and seizing on the
    ball
He marched the penal paces back and suddenly let
    fall
His radiant whiskers, tearing off his nobby coat
    and vest,

And there appeared a mighty "Y" resplendent on his
  chest.

X

"Ted Coogan!" roared the Eli stands,—for it was
  he in truth—
"Run! Run for Yale!" and Ted called up the vigor
  of his youth
And ran a hundred metres with his first pin in his
  teeth,
And Skones and Skreys came down en masse and crowned
  him with a wreath.

A New Sensation

I

The Robber-baron Schnitzelbank
Blasphemed a dreadful swear.
He rant his blond moustaches and
He tore his saffron hair.
For Schnitzelbank was *bored,* and hence
This bellicose despair.

II

His amours had been numberless—
French, German, Swiss, and Dutch;
He'd trifled with the Lorelei,
The Valkyrie, and such.
And nothing of the feminine
Could now enthrall him much.

III

"To horse! To arms!" the Baron bawled.
"I crave a new sensation!
The woods are full of damozels

Who've suffered tribulation
From dragons, robbers, Gott knows what,—
We'll go to their salvation!"

IV

Whereat he spurred his Flemish steed,
At rest his spear he laid,
And all his knights rode after him,
A noble cavalcade! And
All the folk of Schnitzelbank
Laid low and were afraid.

V

Full suddenly they spied a dame
With fourteen lusty babies.
"Od's Blood! Make way!" the Baron cried,
"Don't gawk and stare like gabies!"
And Schnitzelbank frothed and foamed
As if he had the rabies.

VI

But nothing quoth the little dame,
Nor paid the least attention.
To block the daughty Baron's way
Was clearly her intention.
And oh the things the Baron said,
I'd hardly dare to mention.

VII

"Hell's Fire!" he screamed, and couched his lance,
"Shall Schnitzel be thus thwarted?
Charge, Varlets!" yelled the crusty knight,
Or so it was reported.
And quickly the lady turned on him
And with some heat retored:

VIII

"You Broadway comic-opera thief,

Your acts are a disgrace!
Learn to respect a widow's might,
And know your humble place!"
And reaching through the horse's mane,
She slapped the Baron's face!

IX

Appalled, the Baron's escort shook,
Grew pale, turned tail, and fled.
"A new sensation!" Quoth the knight,
And turned exceeding red.
"O lady, worthy Baroness,
Wouldst thou the Baron wed?"

X

The rest is brief; the pair was wed.
From wicked ways and rude.
The Baron, hitherto unscathed,
Was thoroughly subdued.
And dwelt a henpecked father to
The widow's stalwart brood.

A Valentine For Mr. Copeland*

Chambered Nautilus of Hollis
    When you'd play the lover's part
Do you find sufficient solace
    for your heart?

Don't your acolytes distress you,
    In their circle Johnsonese?
Vying which shall cry "God bless you!"
    When you sneeze.

Does your fancy scorn the Present
    When your chorus leaves at last?

* *Professor Charles Townsend Copeland of Harvard University.*

Do you flirt with ladies pleasant
  From the Past?

In your chamber, dim and lonely,
  Swept by each December gale,
Is there none to love you, only
  Mrs. Thrale?

Does the shade of Fanny Kemble
  Share your waking dreams tonight?
Copey, prithee don't dissemble—
  Is it right?

Show some living maid your pity,
  Make her happy past her hope;
Here's her health—the lovely, witty,
  Mrs. Cope!

Wanderlust

By the trackless shores of the sea, where the alien
  shouting of breakers
Beats on a desolate land, and is lost in the swirl
  of the dunes,—
The unsatisfied souls of the sea-dead wander the
  flowerless acres,
Tracing in shadowless sand their mystic ineffable
  runes.
For the sea calls to go forth to the sea and the
  world's far ending,
And the gull's cry carries the sound of gongs from
  the temples of Ind,
And the phantoms of wanderers suffer from lust and
  desire unending,
Luring with scent of strange flowers caught in the
  hair of the wind.

O call of our Mother and Bride, fierce Earth that
    entices with danger,
Whose kiss is a Pain and a Torture, whose passion
    is ultimate Death!
I follow thee Eastward alone, with a love that is
    wilder and stranger
Than that of the dead who have mingled their breath
    with the flame of thy breath.
The wrath of the sea is thy robe, and thy breasts
    are the measureless mountains,
And the fire of thy spirit burns hot in the sullen
    red heart of the East;
Thy whisper is fraught with the laughter of birds
    and the murmur of fountains,
And the vagabond sons of men throng glad to the joy
    of thy feast.

Welsh Song

Oh I sat by a wayside on Cairn-y-brain
To rest my weary feet-o
And a dark-eyed lass came along in the rain
And gave me greeting sweet-o.
A slim Welsh lass on Carn-y-brain
That gave me greeting sweet.

Said I "Will ye sit here beneath my tree;
For the rain is in your hair-o"
So she came and sat on the lap of me
And O but she was fair-o.
And I kissed her full lips tenderly
Nor did she seem to care.

But wae! I felt in my mickle seat
A brogilly pricklin' pain-o
And I leaped full up on my weary feet
And spilled her out in the rain-o

For a red ant-hill had been my seat
On the heights of Cairn-y-brain.

Then I doffed my kilties before the lass
In the braw and gawmy weather
And I rolled about on the dewy grass
An' the balmy purple heather—
O she ran away in the rain, alas!
An' we'll naemore be together!

O the miles are long to my weary feet
And there's many a tempting braeside
But I'd rather lack my bread and meat
Than sit again by the wayside.
Oh nevermore will I take my seat
By the bonny Cymric wayside.

Fragment of a Love Song

Through the thrum of the sleeping city
The desolate tap of a lonely tread
Surged in the darkness wearily-tawdrily,
Like an old timeless song long-sped
From the hurdy gurdies of the dead.

From the window into the alley
Hung I and dropped on timorous feet,
Crouched in the shadow breathlessly, listening,
Waiting the pass of the watchman's beat
And his monstrous shadow on the street.

Crushed once more in my arms her tresses
Full of a thousand shadows of scent,
Full of a nameless rustling, whispering,
Voices of sorrow and laughter blent
And the hot fervor of passion unspent.

The Wanderer to His Heart's Desire

There you—here I;
Not all the sweetness of your face,
Nor joy of your fair company,
Can bring us to one place.

I think of you—
A picture framed in sombre trees,
Eyes where a gleam of sky breaks through
Grey days on summer seas.

The Western wind
That runs the prairie like a flame,
Bears in his fragrant garments twined
A whisper of your name.

In some far land,
When I desire your comradeship
And the cool frankness of your hand,
The sweetness of your lip,

Then do you send
A blown kiss in the wind's long hair;
And though I sleep at the world's end
Yet will it find me there.

The Foundations of a Skyscraper

Ghastly the pit with thousand-candle flares
Sharp as a sword—white, cold and merciless.
Bared to the world, the rock's swart nakedness—
Shadows, and mouths of gloom, like dragon's lairs;
Thunder of drills, stiff spurting plumes of steam,—
Shouts and the dip of cranes, the stench of earth,—
Blinded with sweat, men give a vision birth,
Crawling and dim, men build a dreamer's dream.

Clamor of unknown tongues, and hiss of arc
Clashing and blending; screech of wheel on wheel,—
Naked, a giant's back, tight-muscled, stark,
Glimpse of mighty shoulder, etched in steel.
And over all, above the highest high,
A phantom of fairtowers in the sky.

Hoar Exiles

(An unpublished fragment)

Hoar Exiles, dream you yet of that far time
When proudly strong, you raised your royal crests
Straight to the sun, and splendid in your power
Transcended earth, fit thrones for eagles nests?

The solemn forest, hushed in aged rest
Betrayed no sound save its own whisperings
Stretching forever toward the distant West
Part of th' eternal solitude of things

No man disturbed; but once from out the night
An Indian runner crept from lands afar
Rested a space, then hurried on
With tidings summoning strange tribes to war.

Mayhap, deep in the silent, ancient wood
The Dryads wove their mystic pagan dance
Before Spring dawns, and Pan with Dorian mood
Swayed the mad measures till the day's advance.

Gone is the glory of that golden dream
Gone is the wood that lay toward the West
Now through the streets, the street lamp's
        sickly beam
Strikes the old Dryads head against your breast

Sad was the hour, when leaping to gale
You saw far out to sea across the night
The gleam of lanterns on a plunging sail
The first dim flame of Freedom's beacon light.

Noon

Swirl and pass of listless eyes,
    Thronging up the breathless street;
Clang and roar of iron wheels
    In the midday heat.

Nervous noon-tide whistles shrill,
    Stabbing through the sullen air;
Hoarse, defiant, like a voice
    Dauntless in despair.

See! Against the blinding sky,
    High above the steel-shod hoofs,
Moving wisps of coloring
    On the factory roofs.

Waving arms and streaming hair,
    Joyous leaping, hand in hand,
Sweat-shop girls with lifted face
    Dance a saraband.

Not a tap of rhythmic feet,
    Not a shred of melody,
Lilting thinly on the height,
    Flutters down to me.

Whirling dust of city streets,
    Recklessly they laugh on high;
Tiny notes across the sun
    Dancing in the sky!

Deep-Water Song

The bounding deck beneath me,
    The rocking sky o'erhead,
White, flying spume that whips her boom,
    And all her canvas spread.

Her topmast rakes the zenith,
    Where planets shoal and spawn,
And to her stride God opens wide,
    The storm-red gates of dawn!

Then walk her down to Rio,
    Roll her 'cross the line;
Chinese Joe's a-tendin' door
    Down to Number Nine.
Deep they lie in every sea,
    Land's End to the Horn—
For every sailorman that dies
    A sailorman is born.

Along the battered sea-wall,
    Our women in the rain
Full wearily have scanned the sea
    That brings us not again.

Oh, I'll come home, my dearie—
    Aye, one day I'll come home,
With heaped-up hold of Spanish gold
    And opals of spun foam.

Then walk her down to Frisco,
    Lay her for Hong-Kong;
Reeling down the water-front
    Seven hundred strong
Deep they lie in every sea,
    Land's End to the Horn—
For every sailor-man that dies
    A sailorman is born.

Tall, languid palms that glimmer,
    Blossoms beyond belief,
Sea-gods at play in shouting spray
    On sun-splashed coral reef.

O falling star at twilight,
    O questing sail unfurled
Through unknown seas I follow these
    Down-hill across the world.

Then walk her down to Sydney
    Through to Singapore;
Dutch Marie and Ysobel
    Waitin' on the shore.
Deep they lie in every sea,
    Land's End to the Horn—
For every sailorman that dies
    A sailor man is born.

Sangar

To Lincoln Steffens

Somewhere I read a strange, old, rusty tale
Smelling of war; most curiously named
"The Mad Recreant Knight of the West."
Once, you have read, the round world brimmed with hate,
Stirred and revolted, flashed unceasingly
Facets of cruel splendor. And the strong
Harried the weak . . .

                    Long past, long past, praise God
In these fair, peaceful, happy days.

                                        The Tale:

Eastward the Huns break border,
    Surf on a rotten dyke;

They have murdered the Eastern Warder
    (His head on a pike.)
"Arm thee, arm thee, my father!
    "Swift rides the Goddes-bane,
"And the high nobles gather
    "On the plain!"

"O blind- world-wrath!" cried Sangar,
    "Greatly I killed in youth,
"I dreamed men had done with anger
    "Through Goddes truth!"
Smiled the boy then in faint scorn,
    Hard with the battle-thrill;
"Arm thee, loud calls the warn horn
    "And shrill!"

He has bowed to the voice stentorian,
    Sick with thought of the grave—
He has called for his battered morion
    And his scarred glaive.
On the boy's helm a glove
    Of the Duke's daughter—
In his eyes splendor of love
    And slaughter.

Hideous the Hun advances
    Like a sea-tide on sand;
Unyielding, the haughty lances
    Make daughty stand.
And ever amid the clangor,
    Butchering Hun and Hun,
With sorrowful face rides Sangar
    And his son. . .

Broken is the wild invader
    (Sullied, the whole world's fountains);
They have penned the murderous raider
    With his back to the mountains.

Yet tho' what had been mead
    Is now a bloody lake,
Still drink swords where men bleed,
    Nor slake.

Now leaps one into the press—
    The Hell 'twixt front and front—
Sangar, bloody and torn of dress
    He has borne the brunt.
"Hold!" cries "Peace! God's Peace!
    "Heed ye what Christus says—"
And the wild battle gave surcease
    In amaze.

"When will ye cast out hate?
    "Brothers—my mad, mad brothers—
"Mercy, ere it be too late,
    "These are sons of your mothers.
"For sake of Him who died on Tree,
    "Who of all Creatures, loved the Least,"—
"Blasphemer! God of Battles, He!"
    Cried a priest.

"Peace!" and with his two hands
    Has broken in twain his glaive.
Weaponless, smiling he stands
    (Coward or brave?)
"Traitor!" howls one rank, "Think he
    "The Hun be our brother?"
And "Fear we to die, craven, think ye?"
    The other.

Then sprang his son to his side,
    His lips with slaver were wet,
For he had felt how men died
    And was lustful yet;
(On his bent helm a glove
    Of the Duke's daughter,

In his eyes splendor of love
        and slaughter)—

Shouting, "Father no more of mine!
        "Shameful old man—abhorr'd
"First traitor of all our line!"
        Up the two-handed sword.
He smote—fell Sangar—and then
        Screaming, red, the boy ran
Straight at the foe, and again
        Hell began . . .

Oh, there was joy in Heaven when Sangar came.
Sweet, Mary wept, and bathed and bound his wounds,
And God the Father healed him of despair,
And Jesus gripped his hand, and laughed and laughed. . .

Revolt

Lovers anaemic and spotless;
        Passion deplored as a vice;
Good taste, forsooth, as a ringer for Truth—
        Right,—to be bought at a price.
Peace,—for we fear to do battle,
        Calm,—for it's childish to rage,
Sane Common Sense, while we sit on the fence,—
        God! What a virtuous age!

Youth that is thrifty of comfort,—
        No one who dares be a fool,—
Careful to act with discretion and tact,
        Youthful according to rule.
Drink,—if you take it in season,
        Women,—you know,—in their place;
No harm in Thought if you think what you're taught,—
        Yes, a magnificent race.

Church of the Negative Virtues,—
    Clergymen graceful and "nice,"
Irreproachable quite, talking Sweetness and Light,
    And full of fraternal advice.
Comfortable feeling on Sunday,—
    Nothing unpleasant or odd,—
How sweet for us all to be under the thrall
    Of a socially possible God.

Governed, policed, and upholstered,
    Well-trained, ungracious and hard;
Free to be true, to remake or undo,
    With Beauty and Liberty barred.
Silent, where shouting is glorious,
    In reverence, vulgar and loud,
Vain of a creed that is rotten with greed,—
    A People resurgent and proud.

Oh, there is peace in wrong-doing,
    Joy in the blasphemous thing,
Sweet is the taste of a prodigal waste,—
    Lawless the songs that we sing.
And you, who are holy, have made it,—
    Have ticketed men and their ways,—
Have taken the zest from all that was best
    In these contemptible days!

A Friend

With tossing plumes wind-flung
And princely blazonings,
Days change and end,—
Nights pale and wane—all things

Are as a song once sung,
Save only you, my Friend.

I have not seen your face,
Nor heard your voice, nor known
The touch of you,—
Yet we are closer grown
In many a quiet place
Than lovers ever grew.

Sometime, somewhere, you'll come,
Clean-eyed from wandering
The world's highways,
Brown with suns' weathering,
With wonder-laughter dumb,—
O Friend of all my days!

A Song For May

It seems I have not breathed till now,
Nor felt such deep and still delight;
The wind's a cool hand on my brow,
And I am robed in night—
In high and lordly night.

I want not gold nor silken grace,
Nor to be straw to men's desire;
I'd clasp again my mother's face
Before the evening fire—
The warm, transfiguring fire.

I want not love—alas, I hear
His running feet along the strand—
Ah, woe is me! I fear, I fear
My lover's burning hand—
His hot and eager hand!

The Wedding Ring

"And what is this you offer me?" quoth Love.
A girdle of Red Gold.
And "Gold!" sneered Love in scorn
    (Eyes raining lightnings down)
"Gold!
Am I so tinsel-worn
As to be bought and sold
    Like a woman of the town?"

"But why the Ring?" he queried, wondering.
To bind you in the Law.
"Bind *me*!" cried Love, full loud,
    (A flame of wrath in his hair)
"Law!
Am I so feeble-bowed
That you must burn me raw
    With chains, to keep me there?"

" "Twixt man and maid?" asked Love, incredulous.
Aye—for mayhap you die.
"Die, I!" . . . Love spurned the thing,
    (Flushing imperially)
"Die!
May . . . these that use a Ring
To link them in a lie
    Surely deserve not me!"

The Minstrel of Romance

Strum! Strum! Strum! Strum!
Torches guttering, pennons fluttering,
    Lances glittering in the night!

At a spiking trot, down from Camelot,
    Rideth Lancelot to the fight!
Merrily, merrily, merrily chants
The Minstrel of Romance.

Strum! Strum! Strum! Strum!
Fades the serious world imperious,—
    All that weary us are no more,
Love is wonderous, Life is thunderous,
    Who shall sunder us evermore!
Merrily, merrily, merrily chants
The Minstrel of Romance!

Strum! Strum! Strum! Strum!
End to maundering; Youth a-squandering,
    Let's be wandering wind-swept seas—
White arms amorous, battles clamorous,
    Cities glamorous—sing us these!
Merrily, merrily, merrily chants
The Minstrel of Romance!

Tamburlaine

An Organ Prelude

A voiceless shaking of the air . . .
Then a low shuddering of sound
Vibrant, thunderous, like the profound
Pulsation of great wings. O rare—
In the high-vaulted transept's gloom
Wakes sonant echoing, and the deep
Tone-breakers gather ponderously and leap
From beam to beam, like sullen boom
Of lazy summer thunder. *See!*
On the bare rock-rimmed Scythian plain

The swarthy shepherd Tamburlaine . . .
Swells the great organ suddenly
Steady, glorious, like a galleon flinging
Leeward the roaring foam—and swift
The soaring organ-voices lift,
Terrible as a Crusade singing!
"Tamburlaine! Tamburlaine! Tamburlaine!
Doom of the world's Emperors!
O living Pestilence of Wars,
Thou art God's Scourge, O Tamburlaine'."
Loosed are the shrill, the high pipes' throats,
Joyful the bright gold trumpets blare,
Brazen his monstrous armies flare,
Ruthless his red gonfalon floats!
War! Full-throated, the shattering
Great pipes tumultous give tongue—
Each bar a butchered city sung,
And every chord a slaughtered king!
The flame of cities has scorched God's face,
Murder has made a marsh of the world
Purged with destruction—and down-hurled
Rot the world's tyrants. . . .Lo! the bass:
"God's lash is bloody, Tamburlaine.
Break, heart—die, Emperor of Kings.
Tool of divine and awful things
Too near to godhead, Tamburlaine!"
Falls like a sea-wind at sundown
The full-toned sonorous battle-chant;
Yet the sound-surf reverberant
Rolls the dim-springing nave adown,
Rolls thunderous—subsiding—low—
In a burnt, treeless land where loom
The world's high mountains, lies a tomb—
Vibrant the shuddering tremolo—
A tomb half hid with drifting sand,
Nameless—in Samarkand. . . .

To My Father

That all this lordly pageantry shall glow
When we are gone! That ever the slow
Unchanging earth shall blunder into space
Magnificent with stars! I shall forget your face—
But day and night, like ocean-waves upcurled,
Rhythmic shall foam upon the world.
O wonder, wonder, wonder!
These mantled mountains crowned with thunder,
That diadem of peaks across the East
Where his eyes rested—nought of these has ceased;
And the serene—sea-wind of summer nights
Is a cool hand in lovers' hair (Ah lights
That now are darkness to him!) Flowers and flowers
Rose after rose; high, heavy-scented, towers
The royal magnolia; and the golden-glow;
That had not bloomed before we missed him so,
Is now a yellow flame.

        Calm he lives there,
In the brave armor he alone could bear,
With a proud shield of Honor at his side,
And a keen sword of Wit. And when the tide
Mysterious—when the swift, exultant Spring.
Thrills all this hillside with awakening,
Wild-flowers will know and love him, blossoming.

THE
DAY IN BOHEMIA

or

LIFE AMONG THE ARTISTS

Being a *jeu d'esprit* containing Much that is Original and Diverting.
In which the Reader will find the Cognomens and Qualities of
many Persons destined one day to adorn the Annals of Nations,
in Letters, Music, Painting, the Plastic Arts, and even Business;

TOGETHER WITH

Their Foibles, Weaknesses, and Shortcomings.

And some Account of the Life led by

Geniuses in Manhattan's

QUARTER LATIN

PROPITIATORY.

Who but the veriest Thersites
Would celebrate two Aphrodites?

LADIES, I humbly lay this lay before you,
Its many faults I hope you'll not be hard on
Merely because I failed to underscore you,
(for which I most sincerely beg your pardon)
You'll note, perhaps, a dearth of women,—
I didn't dare put more of them in. . . . . .

The most ru-di-men-tar-y education
Instils the Trojan lady-killer's fate;
So, with considerable trepidation
I would a single goddess celebrate.
And Atlanta's last pursuit
Shows how a nymph will fall for fruit.

If *re* MISS TARBELL, you're inclined to carp.
At these my sentiments, or their veracity
Then notice that she animates my harp
Only in her professional capacity.
(Though I admit, upon reflection,
A tenderness in that direction)

Yet, tho' by exercising due discretion
I hope a Nine Years Warfare to forestall,
I trust I'm culpable of no suppression;—
Cannot these sentiments embrace you all?
These, LADIES! And I hope you've found
Apples enough to go around.

One of Us;
The Only Man
Who Understands My Arguments.

STEFFENS, I hope I am doing no wrong to you
By dedicating this doggerel song to you;
P'raps you'll resent The implied compliment,
But light-hearted liberty seems to belong to you.

Yes, my Bohemian picture's satirical,—
Method of drawing it wholly empirical,—
But there's anaemia
Ev'n in Bohemia,
That there's not more of it—*there* is the miracle!

Even in artists I notice a tendency
To let old Daily Bread gain the ascendancy,
Making that petty boss
Sort of a Setebos
'Stead of a useful but servile despondency.

How can an artist create his Utopia
With his best eye on the World's cornucopia?
See, for example;
There's recompense ample
In just writing this—let us call it—*epopaen.*

Not that we should be *too* earnest,—assumin' us
Free to pursue all the gods that illumine us,—
I don't mean to say
If I had my way
I'd make every man *beautontimorumenos!*

Yet without seeming too greatly didactical,

53

Would I could find the means moral and tactical
To put to rout,
With one hearty shout,
That bane of America, Art that is Practical!

Well, if these numbers recall a good year to you,
And, as to me, certain things that are dear to you,
Take them, you're welcome,
I'm with you till Hell come,
Friend Steffens, consider me quaffing a beer to you!

PREFATORY.

If I've apologies to make
I shall not make 'em.
Nor, if I'm guilty of mistake,
Need you revenge prepare to take;
I'll simply cry "pax tecum!"
No! If excuses I've to name
I *will not* make 'em.

And I refuse to slavishly
Placate the Critic.
No flowery hyperbole
Will ever emanate from me,
Or sentiment politic;—
I really must refuse to be
So parasitic.

To all whose names this lay adorn
I doff my bonnet.
But I will treat with proper scorn,
All affidavits *contra* sworn,
You many depend upon it:—
All those whose names this lay adorn
Insisted on it!

54

THIS DAY IN BOHEMIA

Muse, you have got a job before you,—
Come, buckle to it, I implore you.
I would embalm in deathless rhyme
The great souls of our little time:
Inglorious Miltons by the score,—
Mute Wagners,—Rembrandts, ten or more,—
And Rodins, one to every floor.
In short, those unknown men of genius
Who dwell in third-floor-rears gangreneous,
Reft of their rightful heritage
By a commercial, soulless age.
Unwept, I might add,—and unsung,
Insolvent, but entirely young.

Twixt Broadway and Sixth Avenue,
And West perhaps a block or two,—
From Third Street up, and Ninth Street down,
Between Fifth Avenue and the Town,—
Policemen walk as free as air,
With nothing on their minds but hair,
And life is very, very fair,
In Washington Square.

Bohemia! Where dwell the Sacred Nine,
Who landed, steerage, from the White Star Line,—
(For, when the Sacred Springs dried up in Italy
They packed their duds and emigrated prettily.
And all the Ladies, donning virile jeans,
Became the Editors of Magazines,)

Bohemia! There, hiding neath the Arch,
Acteon on Diana steals a march;
Glimpsing the Huntress at her weekly tub
In the round fountain near the Little Club.
(She with a watchful eye out for the cop
Who haunts the corner where the busses stop.)
Or Dionysus, prone from many dreams,

Praises the vine in gulping dithyrambs;
Till some official Pentheus, billy drawn,
Fans the loud-cursing God, and bids him "On!"
While that old Macnad, with disordered hair,
Each Sabbath eve careens around the Square.

Beneath the trees, when summer-nights are hot,
Bray shawn and psaltery, if you will or not;
Out swarm light-hearted Dagos by the millions
Gay Neapolitans and dark Sicilians—
Shouting and laughing, slowly they creep on
Like a drab frieze about an East Side Parthenon!

Say! unenlightened bards whom I deride,
Defend you Gramercy or Morningside,
As fitter spots for poets to reside?
Nay, you know not where Virtue doth abide!
De GLACKENS, FRENCH, WILL IRWIN linger there?
Nay, they would scorn your boasted Uptown, sir!
Are marble bathtubs your excuse ingenious?
In God's Name, what are bathtubs to a genius!
What restaurant have you that to compare is
With the cool garden back of PAGLIERI'S?
I challenge you to tell me where you've et
Viands more rare than at the LAFAYETTE!
Have you forgot the BENEDICK,—the JUDSON,
(Purest of hostelries this side the Hudson)
The Old BREVOORT, for breakfast late on Sunday,
The CrullERY, where poor men dine on Monday?
You don't remember THOMPSON STREET. For shame!
Nor WAVERLY PLACE, nor, (classic, classic name!)
MACDOUGAL ALLEY, all of stables built,
Blessed home of Art and MRS. VANDERBILT.

> Young Smith he took a studio,—
>   With a fol de rol de rero.
> He sculped like Michael Angelo,—
>   With a rol de rero.
> The neighbors shook their heads and said
> "It's much too much like Rodin's,—

"And then it can't be Art, because
  "It's nothing like St. Gaudens!"
With a rol de rol de rol de rol—
O many a clever rally
Takes place among the geniuses
In bold MacDougal Alley!

Smith felt his life in twain was rent,
  With a fol de rol de rero.
But not his artistic temperament,—
  With a fol de rero.
And so he gave up Art because
  Success you can't rely on,
And up and eloped with a painter's wife
  And now's a social lion!
With a rol de rol de rol de rol—
No one knows who's whose Sally,
The spice of Life's uncertainty
In gay MacDougal Alley!

Lives there a man with soul so dead, I ask,
Who in an attic would not rather bask
On the South side, in lofty-thinking splendor.
Than on the North Side grow obese and tender?
The North Side, to the golden ladle born,
Philistine, suckled at a creed outworn!
Unnumbered Jasons in their motor-cars
Pass fleeceward, mornings, puffing black cigars—
We smoke Fatimas, but we ride the stars!

True to our Art, still there are variations,
Art cannot flourish on infrequent rations;
We condescend to work in humbler sort,
For Art is long and money very short.
Hence it is not so terribly surprising
That ANDREWS deigns to scribble advertising;
ROGERS, whose talent is of epic cast,
At Sunday-paper stuff is unsurpassed.
LEE teaches in an Art School he abhors,

And LEWIS tries to please the editors;
BOB EDWARDS, when he needs some other togs,
Draws pictures for the clothing catalogues.
And I, myself, when no one wants my rhymes,
Yes, even I relax a bit at times.

Yet we are free who live in Washington Square,
We dare to think as Uptown wouldn't dare,
Blazing our nights with arguments uproarious;
What care we for a dull old world consorious
When each is sure he'll fashion something glorious?
Blessed art thou, Anarchic Liberty
Who asketh nought but joy of such as we!

O Muse, inflate your pulmonary bellows
And sing ROG, ANDY, OZ, and all the other fellows
Homage to FORTY-TWO, Parnassus Flats!
Hail to its Cock-roaches, its Dust, its Rats,
Lout your Greek bonnet, to the third-floor-back,
Hymn the two landladies, red-haired and black—
The amiable MARIE, the bland ADELE:
Our Spanish Jack-of-all-work, MANUEL

In winter the water is frigid,
In summer the water is hot;
And we're forming a club for controlling the tub
For there's only one bath to the lot.
You shave in unlathering Croton,
If there's water at all, which is rare,—
But the life isn't bad for a talented lad
At Forty-Two Washington Square!

The dust it flies in at the window,
The smells they come in at the door,
Our trousers lie meek where we threw 'em last week
Bestrewing the maculate floor.
The gas isn't all that it should be
It flickers,—and yet I declare
There's pleasure or near it for young men of spirit
At Forty-Two Washington Square!

But nobody questions your morals,
And nobody asks for the rent,
There's no one to pry if we're tight, you and I
Or demand how our evenings are spent.
The furniture's ancient but plenty.
The linen is spotless and fair,
O Life is a joy to a broth of a boy
At Forty-Two Washington Square!

Third Floor, Hall-room and Back, Elysian bower,
Where the IMMORTAL FOUR spent many a blissful hour!
The high sun-parlor, looking South and East,
Whence we discerned a million cats at least
Communing in the tenement back-yards,
And hove at them innumerable shards.
There spawn the overworked and underpaid
Mute thousands;—packed in buildings badly made—
In stinking squalor penned—and overflowing
On sagging fire-escapes. Such to-and-froing
From room to room we spied on! Such a shrill
Cursing between brass earinged women, still
Venomous, Italian! Love-making and hate;
Laughter, white rage, a passionate debate;
A drunken workman beating up his wife;
Mafia and Camorra,—yelling strife!
The wail of children,—dull monotonous,
Unceasing,—and a liquid, tremulous
High tenor, singing, somewhere out of sight
"Santa Lucia!" in the troubled night.

Below's the barren, grassless, earthen ring
Where Madame, with a faith unwavering
Planted a wistful garden every spring,—
Forever hoped-for,—never blossoming.
Above, th' eternal washing droops in air,
From wall to window hanging, everywhere!
What poet would not yield to their allure
'The short and simple flannels of the poor!'

SHELLEY.

Like battle-riven pennants fluttering,
Float on the serene and variable air
The many-tinted wash. How fair a thing
Is linen cleansed! How virginally fair
Those clinging sunlit draperies! O where
In the vast awful void where slaves are
Hurled headlong into the caverns of despair,
Are such undaunted oriflammes unfurled?
Cringe, tyrants! Hellas flaunts her linen to
the world!

MAURICE MAETERLINCK

A Play in One Act

Persons in the Play:

A Beggar
A Blind Beggar
A Blind Deaf Beggar
A Blind Deaf Dumb Beggar
A Blind Deaf Dumb Crippled Beggar

Beggar—The wash is hung on the clothes line. It
flutters in the wind. It is colored like the
rainbow—red, pale blue, purple. It flutters
like—(He hesitates, pausing)
B.B.—Like wash on a clothes line.
B.—(Simply)—Yes. . . .
B.D.B.—What did you say? I cannot hear. I know
you said something. . . . (Pause)
B.B.—I sense wash on the clothes line. I sense a
red undershirt. Is there a red undershirt?
B.—Yes, a red undershirt with a green patch. And a red—
B.D.B.—What did you say? I know you said something . . .
B.D.D.B.—(Talking with his fingers)—I am afraid.
I am afraid . . .

B.—*Hush! Not so loud. Someone might hear.*
B.D.B.—*I know you said something . . .*
B.B.—*Is there a blue petticoat?*
B.—*Yes and a pair of blue—*
B.D.D.B.—*(Talking with his fingers)—I am afraid . . .*
B.D.D.C.B.—* . . . .*

Slow Curtain.

KEATS.

Thalia, breathe in mine enraptured ears
Strains honey-sweet as lovely Dian hears,
Wrapped in perfumed dusk at Ephesus;
Fire me to sing the vision curious
Fronting my casement. Woven phantasies
Yield to caresses of each wanton breeze;
Here, linen mellowed by the lapse of time,
Wooled in Damascus. From exotic clime
Bandannas pied, and underclothing bright
With Tyrian dye-stuffs; table-cloths once white
Now tinct with lucent syrops of the East
And souvenirs of many a Dago feast. . . . .
Holes, ravels, patches, jauntily displayed,
Fit queenly robes for King Cophetua's beggar maid!

WALT WHITMAN.

Wash! Flung to the four winds of Manahatta,
I Walt Whitman, see this.
The simple, democratic wash of my camerados—
Italianos, Muscovites, and even Americanos—
Undershirts, underdrawers, kimonos, socks, bedclothes,
    pajamas;
Pink, red, green, of various tints, shades and colors;
Some with holes in them, some without holes in them;
Tattered, faded, patched, the Female's equally with
    the Male's I sing!

APOLLO'S beams our humble house adorn

And wake th' IMMORTAL FOUR on Tuesday morn;
Coincident, while still our ears we pound,
The loud alarm-clock gives a horrid sound.
With one bound, orient OSGOOD hits the floor,
(Cerberean timeclocks guard his office door).
REED, with a countenance whence joy has fled,
Drags the resisting ROGERS from his bed.
But ANDREWS still the downy pillow presses,
While every feature deep disgust expresses;
And ere he once forsakes his virgin couch,
Accumulates his early morning grouch.
The radiant OSGOOD round the chamber passes,
Scanning himself in all the looking-glasses;
And whispering that beauty is no shame
Loudly begins to carol "La Boheme."
("O chop it!" ANDY cries "In God's sweet Name!")
Thrice turns the tap, thrice finds the water wanting—

REED excavates a pitcher, nothing daunting,
And, naked, rushes down two flights of stairs,
The cynosure of maiden-ladies' glares.
Then comes the water, mixed with earth and rock,
Belching and bubbling like the Jabberwock,
Like coffee to the sight—but not to taste;
Blaspheming, BELVIDERE remounts in haste,—
Again doth ROGERS in his nest recline,
And must be thence propelled upon his spine,
While STEEL-TRAP ANDY still remains supine.

Now OZZY'S toilet-table stands displayed,
Each silver box in mystic order laid;
In neat pajamas, first the Youth adores
With head uncovered, the cosmetic powers.
EROS' own image in the glass appears,
To that he bends, to that his eyes he rears;
Unnumbered treasures ope at once, and here
The various offerings of the world appear:
This casket India's glowing gems unlocks,
And all Arabia breathes from yonder box.

The tortoise and the steel-works do unite
To make these razors, sabre-edged and bright;
Here, neckties are in brilliant rows arrayed,
Here, powders, patches, pincers and pommade.
Now awful beauty puts on all its arms,—
The fair each moment rises in his charms;
Till, waxing his mustache, at last he turns,
And ardent, for his daily conquests burns!

     Now, when the distant bells are sounding Nine,
Uncoils vast ANDREWS,—hideous, serpentine;
Yawns, blinking, like a famine-stricken owl,
And folds ill-temper round him like a cowl.
"_____ _____ you birds!" he cries "_____
    _____ _____ _____!"
"If I've insomnia, I've got you to thank!
A Business Man has need of peace and quiet;
"Think I can slumber in this _____ _____ riot?
"Three of your collars in my last week's wash;
"This week I find a shirt of REED'S, by Gosh!
"I'm _____ if I will shoulder *your* expense,
"you birds each owe me twenty-seven cents!
"And somebody's been wearing my neckties;
"Why don't you buy things of your own, you guys?"
Robed in a bath-robe like a bagerdine,
Thus ANDY vents his ante-breakfast spleen.
And OSGOOD, chafing 'neath this diatribe,
Forgoes his song, and sharp returns the give:
"Keep your unfashionable clothes apart,
"Who never knew a decent tailor's art!
"Think you I have so very little pride,—
"To let my wash your laundry rest beside?
"By God, in honorable recompense,
"I think *you* owe *us* twenty-seven cents!
"Those neckties, emblems of a bourgeois taste;—
"By God, I wouldn't wear 'em round my waist . . .!"
Etcetera, etcetera, amen!
Until the clocks announce the hour of Ten.

OZZY, who should have been at work by Nine,
Sans breakfast, rushes for the Subway line.
To spend the day foreclosing mortgages,—
Poor widows ruining, with orphans on their knees.
While STEEL-TRAP ANDY, with a ghastly groan
Assumes his pants and seeks the telephone;
Reporting that he is on a business gone,
And has been working in the Bronx since dawn!
Then, with a half pajama for a short,
Splendidly breakfasts at the gay BREVOORT.
REED once more chivies ROGERS from his bed,
And two hours late, goes officeward with dread.

Souls of Scribblers dead and gone,
Where in Hades have ye known
Better wit or worser grub,
Than TOM MASSON'S Dutch Treat Club?
Has the bonehead waiter brought
Chicken-pie, when chops you sought?
For a mess of asphodel
Do they charge so high in Hell?
Bloweth not a double rose
Fairer than the IRWIN BROS.
Nor by other name as sweet
Would be HUGHES or JULIAN STREET!

I have heard that on a day
J. N. FLAGG had stayed away;
If he did, I do declare
Dutch Treat would dissolve in air!
What blithe spirit could be found
To better make the world go round?
Without him how could we face
CHARLIE TOWNE or JOSEPH CHASE?
Who could hear without a sob
All the tales of IRVIN COBB?
Souls of Scribblers dead and gone,
Where in Hades have ye known
Better wit or worser grub

Than TOM MASSON's Dutch Treat Club?

So I arrive at work at half-past-ten,
Sneak to my desk, and madly seize my pen;

Then comes MONACHUS, with his winning smile,
Straightway proposing that we rest a while;
Curses his rheumatism like a Hessian,—
Drinks thirteen cups of water in succession,
Then with closed door we go in secret session.
Allume the fragrant weed! Rest feet on desk!
Work is an eccentricity grotesque!
Dream of the perfect magazine to be!
Condemn our O.F. choice of poetry!
Impugn the literary taste of J. S. P.!
Fashion an age when routine-slaves are free!
To point a tale, to drive dull care away,
NOCKO then reads a bit of Rabelais.
So the time passes, sped with royal fun
Till the white tower booms the stroke of One.

Comes SIDDALL with a cynic lip up-curled,—
SIDDALL, our dormer window on the World!
Kind-eyed behind his glasses, best of friends,
With the World's foibles at his finger-ends.
Roars out a jest, and praises with a damn,
And pricks our bubbles with an eipgram;
SIDDALL, as sensible as he is keen,—
The high-brow low-brow of the Magazine;
"The SPORTING EDITOR has joined the bunch"
Cries he "Here's NORRIS, and it's time for lunch."
Here comes ALB BOYDEN in the King of shirts,
(He is so fashionable that it hurts.
Indeed, in gazing on him, one suspects
That clothes can vanquish physical defects.
So cavalier his air, who would not be him?
Young ladies come from Illinois to see him!)

The rest of us are good at so-and-so,—
But ALB'S the one who makes the wheels to go.
He beats down struggling authors in their price,

Refuses stories with a grace so nice,
That ladies with a Novel (folded flat)
Stay hours in his office for a chat.
Great editor, great hustler through and through,
He has ideas on literature, too!

So We go striding up the Avenue. . . .
At KEEN'S CHOP HOUSE ON Thirty-something Street,
On Tuesday midday we were wont to meet,—
Some for the talk, but most to simply eat,—
The pink of New York's chivalry DUTCH TREAT!
     FLAGG the unflagging, flaunting like a banner,
Carrying manly beauty with a manner!
A dozen masterpieces in each hand,—
(He turns out ten a day, you understand)
Reputed rich beyond the dreams of Art,
Yet democratic,—with a heart, a heart.
Each look a diamond, every word a pearl,—
Holds men enchanted like a clever girl.
STREET, with a romance on his eyebrow,—TOWNE,
Living the Poet's reputation down;
The ever-gay BILL DALY taking his,
Hellenic hair above an Irish phis;
Two IRWINS (Count 'em,—two) in conversation
Almost as clever as their reputation;
CHARLES DANA GIBSON, prisoned in a collar;
And OWEN JOHNSON, (Price, each word, one dollar);
WOODS-HUTCHINSON, with stories anatomic;
JONES, BURGESS JOHNSON, MASSON, of the Comic;
Old IRVIN COBB, father of mirth Homeric,
Boomer of tales—er, wholly atmospheric;
As full of genial flavor as a tun
Of Rhenish grapes well-ripened in the sun.
Round him reels laughter, with a face of gold,—
And from him flow all stories told or never told!
     Full many others. What things have I seen
Done at the DUTCH TREAT! heard words that have been
So nimble, and so full of subtle flame
As if that every one from whence they came

Had meant to put his whole wit in a jest,
and had resolved to filch from LIFE the best
Of even its dull numbers.

                Thus pleasure we
Then back to work again at half-past three.

Collier's Weekly ran a two-page ad:
"We've tried ten editors, but all were bad,
"For some had principles and some had no,
"And some a sense of humour so they had to go."

Then up spake Hapgood from his office-chair:
"Excuse the freedom, Mr. Coll-i-aire,
"If you want an editor, you bet your bones
"That the man for Collier's is Casey Jones!"

                Chorus:

Casey Jones! Editor of Hampton's:
Casey Jones! And the Cosmopolitan:
Casey Jones! Practical Reformer,
Friend of Mr. Pinchot and a baseball fan.

Said Mister Collier with a dismal frown:
(Or so the typist-lady took it down)
"Has this man Casey any ideas new?"
Said Hap: "He thinks just what you tell him to!"

"Ha, Ha!" cried Collier "I'll search no more,
"Where can I find this perfect editor?"
"He sits a-straddle of a ten-inch gun,
"A-writing yellow headlines for the New York Sun!"

                Chorus:

Casey Jones! etc.
The POETS' HOUR! Round BOYDEN'S desk, at five,
War-grey and stripped for action they arrive.
PHILLIPS, whose judgment we so oft deplore,—
Poet a third, and two-thirds Editor;
Though gentle dreamer, business-man of steel,—
Shooting ideas like sparks from emery wheel,

But totally unable to express them;
We cannot understand his thoughts,—must guess them,
Oraculates,—gesticulates,—in fine
BOYDEN, the high-priest, doth the sense divine!
NOCK, clasping Matthew Arnold to his heart,—
An anarchist in everything but art!
AGRICOLA MINERVA TARBELL;—I,
Rejected verse in hand, and fire in mind eye!
"What's up?" says SIDDALL, nervous "Poetry?
"My God! This is no place for low-brow me!"
            MONACHUS opens: "Verse is our disgrace!
"Where in these days is the true singer's place?
"Sure *ars poetica* is on the wane,—
"This last month's Magazine gives me a pain!"
"It's *my* best choice" says PHILLIPS "What is yours?"
"See Century, Atlantic, or McClure's!"
"Ridiculous!"—"The poets all abhor us!"
"Our verse is rotten!"—NOCK and I in chorus;
REED'S going to cast another pearl before us!"
"I am!" I answer with an angry hiss,
Tapping my poem, "What is wrong with this?"
"THE MINSTREL OF ROMANCE"—"No harmony—"
Cries Nock "Too much *cacoethes scribendi*—"
"Genus irritabile vatum—" "You should read
"Your Matthew Arnold,—" "Arnold! Huh! Indeed!
"A polished, strengthless, sapless, hide-bound bard—"
"Walt Whitman? Hardware cataloguing by the yard—"
"Foot—rhythm—rhyme—stanza—Sapphics—Lessing—Pope—
"Hellenic—Dionysius—couplet—trope—"
"Horace,—" ("Assistance!" cries the SID "Police!")
"Poetic Laws—" (NOCK) "Hold!" says PHILLIPS "Peace!
"Down with the stilted numbers of the Schools!
"For Rules were made for Art, not Art for Rules!
"Poetry is—at least I hold it so"—
"Poetry's—"(gesture), (gesture), "—er—, you know
"NOCK'S THEORY, in short, is full of holes—
"Sir Hudson Maxim or the Reverend Bowles!"
MONACHUS bludgeons us with ancient Greek,
French, Latin, Hebrew,—and I take a sneak,

Most cravenly escaping from the battle
Now raging o'er a phrase of Aristotle!

    Since poesy is dead, in dole
    I'll to come lonely cave;
    And there I swear no more I'll troll
    My mercenary stave.
    Perhaps I'll write a play,
    Or turn to prose instead;
    Unrhythmic is my soul,
    Since po-
    Since po-a, po-a, po-a,
    Poia po-
    Since poesy is dead.

    Calliope is dumb—to scenes
    More happy Pan has hied,—
    So blame it on the magazines
    And lay your pen aside.
    Like Ida M. Tarbell
    A farmer I'll become,
    And cultivate my greens,
    Calli-
    Calli-io, li-io, li-io
    Callio li-
    Calliope is dumb!

    The office wash-room next our **HERO** seeks,
His face he rubs, his wavy hair he sleeks;
Reads once again the scented missive o'er:
"To meet some artist friends,—half after four . . .
"Here at the studio . . . aesthetic tea . . ."
Then down into the Subway hurries he;
Tall, handsome, manly, sureoled like a saint,
Greek-profiled—let's be modest (which he ain't)
And leave his portraiture for other folks who paint

When the world seems a dismal and desolate spot,—
Sing toory-a-loory-a-loodle!
And your pockets are empty, as likely as not,—

Sing toory-a-loory-a-loodle!
Don't jump in the river or drink gasoline,
There'll always be plenty of boodle
For the laziest barty with plenty of nerve
Who makes clever use of his noodle!

Chorus:

To work like a Turk in the sun
Has never impressed me as fun;
And manual labor is ultra-bourgeois,—
I'd rather take mine with a gun,—and run,—
A gentleman's wits are enough
To gain him a wad of the stuff,
And the word of a grafter who knows what he's after
Is Bluff! Bluff! Bluff!

At number _____, (the street I shall not name)
There is a studio, like a hundred same;
Where great UMBILICUS is wont to sit,
Not painting,—simply mouthing over it.
When young, he studied on the Continent,—
Eleven years in galleries he spent
Copied the Masters with minutest care,
Learned what they ate, and how they wore their hair;
Lived a new life where'er he made his home,—
Rembrandt in Holland, Cimabue in Rome,
Velasquez in Madrid, and in abhorrence
Held all but Michaelangelo in Florence;
In Venice, took a palace full of fleas,
And was for all the world like Veronese;
In London, mentioned for the Royal Academy
For so well imitating Alma-Tadema;
Procured a mistress, sported velvet pants,
And imitated everyone, in France
And then, committing all these things to heart,
Further pursued the formulas of Art:
Gave up his pension, starved him in an attic,
Drew Early Saints, in attitudes ecstatic,—
Anemic Christs on an anemic cross,

After the wan Theotocopulos.
Became Pre-Raphaelite, neglected bones,
And painted like a jelly-fish Burne-Jones.
Resuming then his money, jot by tittle,
He joined the Realists in the hospital.
So gradually, curious to relate,—
Beginning spiritual and attentuate,
He grew more colorful the more he ate.
Van Dyck and Titian, Fortuny and Turner,
Furnish in turn the fuel for his burner;
Still, as his appetite and weight increase,
He jumps to Manet, Whistler and Matisse.
At last he knew so much, he was so deft,
That neither vision, fire, nor self was left.
So at the League he finally had the luck ter
Be nominated Critic and Instructor;
Teaching to all this ripe philosophy:
"Art is not Art that cannot published be."

    Sinks then your hand within his soft, white, hand—
"My dear, dear friend! So few who understand . . .!"
And you are in. A lofty, skylit room,
Each window draped, and dusky as a tomb;
On a brass tripod Chinesepunk doth smell,
And scented candles stink and fume as well;
Surely no fresh air ever enters here!
This must be the Artistic Atmosphere.
An easel, where a cryptic canvas lurks,
Conceived in pain, and therefore done in jerks;
A purple maiden, hair of livid green,
Drowned in a red sea, title, "Serpentine."
Another. Lady *couchante,* nude and gory,
Entitled "Nocturne. *Troppo con amore"*;
"Symphony. Sevenths more or less diminished."
And other canvases; but not one finished.
"Nature" he breathes "is never quite complete,
"Would you with Nature wish that Art complete?
"A thing is never finished when you end it.
"Bergson and Heraclitus both defend it;

"Merely conceive,—depict the soul,—suggest,—
"The psychically-perceptive does the rest."
A thumb-and-finger gesture, for to thrill you
With feelings like a Virgin of Murillo.
How can he paint an Idea, as he said,
Without a single Idea in his head?

A clack of squabbling voices smites the ear.
Dim in the murk the other cranks appear;
BUFO, who one short verse per year produces,
Explaining by the following excuses:
"I Youth's sweet-scented manuscript unroll,
"But when the heart's systole and diastole
"O'erflows the well of poetry in my soul."
(BUFO's an Art-for-Art's-sake out-and-outer,—
We're fortunate his well is not a spouter)
SHAEMAS, who out-revives the Celt Revival,—
Considers Synge an upstart and a rival;
TRIMALCHIO, long-haired, who thinks it nice is
That artists should be steeped in all the vices;
And measures such a man, not by his wits,
But by th' atrocities that he commits;
Hates decency as Chibelline a Guelph,—
Not brave enough to either be, himself;
STREPHON, who sings of Youth, And Wind, and Flowers,
And Open Roads, and Vagabonds, for hours;
Cries "Back to Nature," goes without a hat,
And—never stirs from his steam-heated flat!
Anear him CHLOE, in a pastoral dress,—
Which cost at least three hundred flat, I guess,—
Revolves her onyx eyes with some success;
She wields no brush, manipulates no lyre,
Her job in life is simply to inspire.
LILITH, one luring line from lips to limb,
Picks out a man, and plays love-songs to him;
Discussing, meanwhile, in a lower tone,
Free Love, and other fancies of her own;
True, never public hearing has had she,—
(A managerial conspiracy)

They call her the American Chaminade;
But I, who oft have been her Ichabod,
Think it's a case of too much 'spare the rod.'
SPORUS the Anarchist, who as he sips
Delivers us a new Apocalypse;
Although his mouth is for war, his heart's for peace,
He wouldn't feel quite safe without Police.
And here's the RICH MAN, fidgetting beside us;
Who tries to be Maecenas,—and is Midas;
And from his talk, it presently appears
That *every* Midas has an ass's ears!
FLACCUS, whose Scarlet Lettered proboscis
Proclaims to all the world that Gin his boss is,—
(His frescoes are a product of the Gin).
BALBUS, a Socialist from nose to chin;
POPPEA, who paints miniatures on clam-shells,
And should be ostracised by her own damn shells;
BUBO, who sleeps, 'tis rumored, in his shirt,
And thinks that painters should exist in dirt;
And all about, a dozen curious females,
Who would be, and again would never be males;
The mild, the violent, the stout, the thin,—
One cup of Oolong makes the whole crowd kin.

> *The English drink tea in the morning*
> *From Trafalgar Square to Bohee,—*
> *And that ought to be enough warning*
> *To anyone tippling tea*
> *Ah me*
> *To anyone tippling tea.*
> *Far be it from me to be scorning*
> *The Britisher's bold chivalree,—*
> *But the clothing his person adorning,*
> *Ah, that's the result of the tea.*
>
> *I wouldn't for anything tarnish*
> *The fame of the heathen Chinese,—*
> *But note his exterior varnish*
> *Produced by the action of tea*
> *Ah me*

Produced by the action of tea.
And if you think this a bit yarnish,
Consult the Encyclopedea;
It says "If complexion you'd garnish
"Refrain from indulging in tea!"

Anon they worship at the Master's shrine,
Anon they squabble o'er some puling poet's lines;
Wild theories, some brighter thinker's leaving,
They misapply, believing they're believing;
With arguments fantastic and absurd,
Each one attempts to sandwich in a word:
TRIMALCHIO proclaims himself Futurist
Because his works are always judged the poorest;
CHLOE for Bahaism has a passion,
Because,—O well, because it is the fashion;
SHAEMAS opines that straightway bound for Hell is
The man who has not studied Hav'lock Ellis;
While LILITH wants ejected from the house
The vulgar fool who does not care for Strauss;
BUBO'S the literary of the crew
Because he reads the Sunday Book Review;
Of all these cranks whom we have been reviewing
Not one has done a single thing worth doing!

Cranks, cranks, cranks, cranks,—
Blanks, blanks, blanks, blanks,—
Talk about talking and think about thinking,
And swallow each other without even blinking;
A little of Bernardshaw,—not very much of him,—
Ibsen, a modicum—Nietzsche, a touch of him,—
A pinch of Karl Marx,—and a bit of Strindberg,—
And much from the novels got out by McClurg;—
Each woman a parasite,—each man a tank,—
And that is the neo-Bohemian crank.

Dubs, dubs, dubs, dubs,—
Cubs, cubs, cubs, cubs,—
Fixing the world with a cheerful finality,—
Preaching a maudlin Bob Chambers morality;

74

Sore on Society,—won't do a thing to it,—
Willing to sacrifice self,—with a string to it,—
In spite of affecting abhorrence of pelf,
You'll notice that each one is out for himself;
All members of petty aesthetical clubs.—
And these are the neo-Bohemian dubs.

     UMBILICUS now rises and remarks
"HAFIZ, the Prince of Syrio-Persian larks,
"Has deigned to pyricize within our midst;
"Did I proclaim aright?" HAFIZ: "Thou didst;"
"HAFIZ, defier of aesthetic laws,—"
"Bravissimo! Bis! Bis!"—in short, applause.
"*—A tour de force* original, unique,—
"The world's not heard before,—*c'est magnifique!*
" 'Tis called, my friends, "A sonnet in A-Flat'!"
Applause! I stealthily attach my hat,
HAFIZ, a person of the tint of guano,
Makes his way, langorous, to the piano;
With a preliminary coquetry,
His larynx clears, and thumps the A-Flat key.
"O moon of love—" thump! thump! thump! thump! thump! thump!
"O moon of love," HAFIZ is up astump;
"O moon of love," but ere he can repeat it,
I rise up and incontinently beat it!

O to be shut in that seraglio
When through the town the West wind bloweth so!
O to talk pictures in a stinking lair,
When the great City's an intaglio rare
In the clean golden wash of evening air!
O to discuss some minor poet's bleat!
When all about tremendous pulses beat!
O, in a studio to fume and gas,
When in the street such faces pass and pass!

O let some young Timotheus sweep his lyre
Hymning New York. Lo! Every tower and spire
Puts on immortal fire!

This City, which he scorn
For her rude sprawling limbs, her strength unshorn,—
Hands blunt from grasping, Titan-like, at Heav'n.
Is a world-wonder, vaulting all the Seven!
Europe? Here's all of Europe in one place;
Beauty unconscious; yet, and even grace.
Home? Here all that Rome was, and is not,—
Here Babylon,—and Babylon's forgot.
Golden Byzantium, drunk with pride and sin,
Carthage, that flickered out where we begin. . . .
London? A swill of mud in Shakespeare's time;
Ten Troys lie tombed in centuries of grime!
Who'd not have lived in Athens at her prime,
Or helped to raise the mighty walls of Rome?
See, Blind men! Walls rise all about you here at home!
Who would not hear once more
That oceanic roar,
"Ave! Ave Imperator!"
With which an army its Augustus greets?
Hark! There's an army roaring in the streets!
This spawning filth, these monuments uncouth
Are but her wild, ungovernable youth.
But the sky-scrapers, dwarfing earthly things,—
Ah, that is how she sings!
Wake to the vision shining in the sun!
Earth's ancient, conquering races rolled in one,
A World beginning,—and yet nothing done!

     Digressions do no harm, but then this is
A rather serious parenthesis.

     So, to resume our muttons, as they say
Homeward the POET takes his jocund way.
Escaping, with his customary luck,
Full many an over-eager motor-truck.
Harmonious, both his outer man and inner
Proclaim the glad proximity of dinner.
Arrives at FORTY-TWO, runs through the mail
"Ten statements due," but not a sign of kale).

     ROG, wreathed in pipe-smoke, sits upon his seat
Perusing Rum-ti-Foo's great Bishop, Pete,

(Hasn't had time all day, he says, to eat),
ANDREWS, upon whose countenance is blent
Virtue and pride, naive and innocent,
Surveys his conscience pure, and is content
(Two hours upon a certain lounge he spent).
While OSGOOD smiles and sings with joy intense,
Without the least conformity to sense.
"Shall we shog off? No money? There's the rub—"
"I vote" cries ANDY "for the HARVARD CLUB
"One doesn't have to pay there,—one can sign—"
"I'm broke" says REED "The CRULLERY for mine"
Then OSGOOD searches vainly for his wallet,—
PAGLIERI'S seems to tickle OZZY'S palate;
"I've just two bones;" adds ROGERS "without animus
"I move we make the Dago-joint unanimous!"
"The Ayes appear to have it—" "Look who's here
"Colonel BOB HALLOWELL—cheer, soldiers, cheer!
"Boom! Boom! The sunset gun! Our country's banner!
"That martial blush! That military manner!"
The furious HALLOWELL emits a roar,
And bears his cruel tormento to the floor,—
Comes the loud crash of tables toppling o'er.
The man beneath, the family in the attic,
Pound on the steam-pipe a protest emphatic.
This evening there'll be trouble. Never mind
Tonight at any rate we will have dined.
       Just as our forces on the street deploy,
Appear the genial WOLF and SAM McCOY!
Balloon-like, ROGERS bounces on ahead
Then SLOTHFUL SAMUEL, less alive than dead,
OZZY and HERR, with one unmeaning grin,
Talk gibberish you'll find no meaning in.
REED, following, elated and erect,
BOB HALLOWELL,—gloves, hat and all correct.
Old ANDREWS singing harshly,—music wrong,—
Last, like a wounded snake, drags his slow length along.
PAGLIERI'S self directs us, with a leer
To the round table waiting at the rear.

Bring on your wine, bring on your raviola,
Here's EDWARDS and his Kitten—let us troll a
Catch that will ring from Cos Cob to Ecola!

Gaston the Gascon, R. I. P.
An eating house did keep.
His Gallic food was very good,—
His prices were not steep.

He six delicious courses gave
And win, for fifty cents.
And FOUR would come to feed their tum,
But seldom other gents.

They wolfed his bread, they drank his wine,
They called for helpings two.
And nought indeed was left to feed
The cat, when they were through.

They ate the chairs, they ate the plates,
They ate the cat, they say.
Involuntary bankruptcy
Took Gaston Simonet.

HOORAY—RAY—RAY
FOR GASTON SIMONET!.

Italian Paul then took the place,
His face with hope was bright.
When through the door the fateful FOUR
Did loom upon his sight.

He louts him low, he rubs his hands
He leads them to a seat.
"Good customers!" poor Paul avers
Till they begin to eat.

They ate the tables, ate the spoons,
And even ate the trays.
Italian Paul went to the wall
In less than thirty days.

THEN—STAND—UP—ALL
A HEALTH TO DAGO PAUL!

Upon Sixth Avenue there is
A German Delicatessen.
  And there once more the hungry FOUR
Each day are wont to fressen.

O feeble is that hapless joint
And empty is its till;
But I confess uneasiness
That it is going still.

OH—WHAT—A BLESSIN'
A GERMAN DELICATESSEN!

Home through the dingy, white-lit, a clangorous street,
Arms linked, the red wine dancing in our feet;
Past the Jew shoemen stewing in their caverns,
Past the fast-swinging doors of taverns;
Through shabby, work-free crowds adventuring,
Treading like rich men, heads up, arms a-swing,—
Dark sweat-shop girls, harsh-laughing as they go,—
Lovers, bound for the moving-picture show,—
Above, like hammers on the lid of hell,
The nervous, grating thunder of the El.
  Home, with our coats off and our weeds alight,
All windows open to the roaring night;
ANDY and OZZY at their checker game
Squabbling,—at poker SAM and HERR the same;
ROG making observations quite satyric,—
Oblivious REED, at work upon a lyric,—
BOB HALLOWELL, growing dreamier and dreamier
To find himself in actual BOHEMIA!
"Is Mr. REED in?" stand, boys! *Mecum dominus!*
It is the landlady,—her voice is ominous.
She enters; sits; swift falls the buoyant talk;
REED'S limbs atremble,—ANDREWS' face of chalk;
OSGOOD alone his customary verve
Exhibits, and his customary nerve.
"Good evening, Madame!" cries "Well, well, well, well!

"Indeed a pleasure,—more than I can tell—"
With a silk handkerchief dusts off his chair,
His eyes implore her to be seated there!
"I've come—" she says. "Our good-luck that is so"
And OZZY'S bow is worthy of the Beau.
"My lodgers have complained—this afternoon—"
"Ah!" observes OZ "the weather's nice for June,—
"Why then complain?" The dame begins again:
"It is not of the weather they complain—"
Our champion agrees "Nor yet do we,—
"We're satisfied to let the weather be.
"And you, dear Madame? You are feeling tony?
"To that your blooming looks bear testimony!"
She tries once more: "Well, in the room below
"A newly-married couple live, you know—"
"Two-te-twa-twa" sings OZZY "Who'd have thought it—"
"But then, that oughtn't to be talked of, ought it—?"
"And they complain—" "O, go no farther, please,—
"How sad are these unhappy marriages—"
"But—" "You've been married? Happily, I trust?
"Ah well! Earth unto earth, and dust to dust—"
"Then there's the man upstairs—" "What, married too?
"The sly dog! This will never, never do!
"We won't get married after this, eh, boys?—"
Cries Madame "They complain of too much noise!"
"Ah" says defeated OZZY, quite resigned,
"Have you a certain culprit in your mind?"
      She sniffs, and straightway dons a mien of gloom,
While breathlessly we listen to our doom,
"I'm not one who would muzzle without ruth
"The harmful effervescences of Youth—
"I am not one to lightly cry 'Heraus!'
"I want you all contented in my house;
"But I declare it seems a bit too bad
"For those as hadn't PAID to bother those as had!"
Silence; then cometh to our burning ears
Soft sound of sobs, and tink of trickling tears.
She weeps! Milady weeps! Blush, thoughtless boys!
Why in Beelzebub made you that noise?

She's off again "I do not like to say it
"But there's one rule here, and all must obey it;
"Those who have not PAID RENT for half a year
"Must keep the peace—they cannot rough-house here;
"My landlord duns—no cash, you make a racket,—
"My lodgers leave,—I starve"—(ROGERS: *"Hic jacet"*)
Grief incoherent: with a furtive glance
REED searches through the pockets of his pants;
Nothing! He nudges HALLOWELL, who then
Slips him a surreptitious bill of ten.
"Madame" he cries "Accept this little token
"And credit my arrears; in peace unbroken
"From this time on I promise you shall dwell,
"The folks below, and he above, as well!"
Madame arises, smiles, and dries her tears,—
The episode is finished off with cheers.

Artists lodger, be a gent
Pay, O pay to me my rent!
Or, and I will think me blest,
Pay but half and keep the rest!
List, O listen to my prayers
Les affaires sont les affaires!

By my spread of rarest lawn
That you wipe your brushes on;
By the sheets the laundry says
That you use for canvases;
By my stricken hair-cloth chairs
Les affaires sont les affaires!

By the stories that you tell
Of the pictures you will sell
By my furniture you pawn
And the proceeds rollick on;
Pay, or mount no more these stairs
Les affaires sont les affaires!

A knock. 'Tis HIRSCH! His devilish smile says, "Never
"Was anyone so altogether clever!"

Observe his air of "I-am-one-of-you"
Adopted for this babu *milieu;*
That laugh ironic, that superb *sang-froid*
Is like a character from Bernard Shaw;
His critic-analytic turn of mind
Dissects his friends, around, before, behind,—
Then, plumbs itself his intellect profound,
Till the *disjecta membra* strew the ground;
Indeed, so has he analyzed his soul,
That HIRSCH doth never seem entirely whole!
For all of that, a Voice Among the Dumb,
Who will speak great things in the days to come!

        And with him LIPPMANN,—calm, inscrutable,
Thinking and writing clearly,—soundly, well;
All snarls of falseness swiftly piercing through,
His keen mind leaps like lighting to the True;
His face is almost placid,—but his eye,—
There is a vision born to prophecy!
He sits in silence, as one who has said:
"I waste not living words among the dead!"
Our all-unchallenged Chief! But were there one
Who builds a world, and leaves out all the fun,—
Who dreams a pageant, gorgeous, infinite,
And then leaves all the color out of it,—
Who wants to make the human race, and me,
March to a geometric Q. E. D.—
Who but must laugh, if such a man there be?
Who would not weep, if WALTER L. were he?

        A timid footstep,—enter then the eager
KEATS—SHELLEY—SWINBURNE—MEDIAEVAL—
        SEEGER;
Poe's raven bang above BYRONIC brow,
And Dante's beak,—you have his picture now;
In fact he is, though feigning not to know it,
The popular conception of a Poet.
Dreaming, his eyes are steadily alight
With splendors of a world beyond our sight;
He nothing knows of this material sphere,—
Unwilling seems, at times, to linger here;

Beauty is all his breath, his blood, he says,—
Beauty his shrine, and Love its priestesses.
Wildly he talks, with solemn, bell-like voice,
In words that might have been old Malory's choice,—
Proclaiming, in the manner of ascetics,
"For ethics we must substitute aesthetics!"
    Who's this, that like the West Wind, buoyant, free,
Blows in upon us? Sculptor ARTHUR LEE!
Soi-disant superman, and self-styled Lord
Of Sculptors, preaching the inspired Word
Of Modern Art. You cannot hear him speak,—
Epic and dialectic, like a Greek,—
Without believing in his haughty claim
That the round earth will echo to his name.
    The unkempt HARRY KEMP now thumps our door;
He who has girdled all the world and more,
Free as a bird, no trammels him can bind,
He rides a box-car as a hawk the wind;
A rough thin face, a rugged flow of words,—
A Man, who with ideals himself begirds;
Fresh from a fiery ordeal that has paved
The Pit anew—from terrors trebly braved
He rises, burning to avenge the wrong
By flooding all the stupid earth with song.
Here's to you HARRY, in whatever spot!
True Poet, whether writing it or not.

Much have I traveled in the realms of gold,
And many goodly states and kingdoms seen;
Round Western towns and countries have I been
Where bosses fealty to Roosevelt hold.
Oft of one wide expanse had I been told,
That loud Walt Whitman ruled as his demesne:
Yet did I never breathe its pure serene
Till I heard Roget speak profuse and bold:

Then felt I like some lesser Hagedorn
When a new rhyme-tag swims into his ken;—
Or like stout Wheelock on the gladsome morn

When a new book is published,—and his pen
Scribbles another volume yet unborn—
Silent, upon a stool, in Hoboken!

Loud roars the conversation, as Olympus
Roars when the deities convene to gimp us;
KEMP thunders Anarchism, and is wrecked
On a sharp flint from LIPPMANN'S intellect,—
Who Socialism in his turn expounds,
Which LEE declares is founded on false grounds;
ROGERS and HIRSCH with fury fight away
Upon what constitutes a perfect play;
SEEGER and KEMP twang each his lyric lute,
And Poetry disdainfully dispute;
ANDREWS, appealed to, climbs upon the fence,
And all combine, in scorn, to flog him thence.
Poor HALLOWELL'S dilemma is immense;—
Too bold for that, too cautious to be bold,
He hesitates until the subject's cold;
While OSGOOD, WOLF, McCOY DO stand aloof,
Contemptuously watch us raise the roof.
        Now with an easy caper of the mind
We rectify the Errors of Mankind;
Now with the sharpness of a keen-edged jest,
Plunge a hot thunder-bolt in Mammon's breast;
Impatient Youth, in fine creative rage,
With both hands wrests the quenchless torch from Age;
Not as the Dilettanti, who explain
Why they have failed,—excuse, lament, complain,
Condemn real artists to exalt themselves,
And credit their misfortune to the elves;—
But to Gods of Strength make offertory,—
And pit our young wits in the race for glory!
        Perhaps we flay our artists' lack of power,
Or damn with mirth the poets of the hour;
One in particular I call to mind
Who says he's left America behind:—

O let us humb-ly bow the neck

To George Syl-ves-ter Vi-er-eck
Who trolled us a merry little Continental stave
Concerning the Belly and the Phallus and the Grave—

It would have almost raised the hair
Of Oscar Wilde or Bau-de-laire
To hear Mr. Vi-er-eck so frank-ly rave
Concerning the Belly and the Phallus and the Grave—

And in the last an-al-y-sis
He says it nar-rows down to this:
A fig for the favors that the high gods gave!
Excepting the Belly and the Phallus and the Grave—

If you have drunk Life to the lees
You may console yourself with these;
For me, there are some things that I do not crave
Among them the Belly and the Phallus and the Grave—
What ho! for the Belly and Phallus and the Grave
The Belly and the Phallus
And the ballad very gallus
    And the Grave!

It borders midnight! Rattle all the doors,
With the vehemence of the lodgers' snores.
Now one by one the geniuses do yawn,—
Rise up,—deliver parting shots,—are gone.
SEEGER remains. "The LAFAYETTE?" he cries;
"Aye!" (Fevered are our brains, and wide our eyes.)
ANDY alone declines to be seduced
But virtuously prepares him for the roost;
"You squander Youth" says he "In dissipation!"
"For the Wise Man, all things in moderation;
"Efficiency—the Business Man—brain force—"
"Short sport!" we sneer "Conservative,—and worse!"
Singing, the Four went to the LAFAYETTE
Quite like a scene from Murger,—*sans grisette.*

    "You are very well met
    Reed and Osgood and Rogers;
    At the old Lafayette

You are very well met—
Come, set 'em up! Set
'Em up, jolly codgers!
You are very well met
Reed and Osgood and Rogers!"
Round a bare table in the bright cafe
We loll, while wild Italian minstrels play
"You Candy Kid." The flashing demi-monde
Carouses,—laughs,—grows fonder and more fond;
Frenchmen pursue th'eternal game of chess,
Playwrights compose, and bards their woes confess
With a stub pencil on the table-top
(*Chef d'oeuvres* perish with to-morrow's mop)
In a warm glow of Cointreau Triple Sec
REED has a million visions at his beck,
OZZY draws portraits on his unpaid check,
SEEGER draws rhymes from fountains never spent,
While ROGERS purrs, and grins and is content.

REED gapes, OZ gapes, ROG gapes,—and SEEGER gapes,
Dark is the Square,—a few dull huddled shapes
Lie on the grass; a homeless, workless crew.
Chill is the air,—a distant clock strikes two;—
Sharp sounds the late home-comer's step, and deep
Breathes the wide-circled city in its sleep.
There is a slip of moon—Good Nights are said,
And arm-in-arm we stumble home to bed.

But at our door we hesitate, and grin,—
Someone talks on and on and on, within;
Now ANDREWS' voice, uplifted, tries in vain
To dawn the flood,—as he for bed were fain.
'Tis REEVES the Philosoph, who can outpreach a
Young Baptist,—REEVES, the true Blond Beast of Nietzsche!
Our new Freethinker,—to whom all Emotion,
Enthusiasm, Faith, Love, Rage, Devotion,
Etcetera, is positively Boeotian!
Born to propound, unfold a tale, debate,
And charming, if he would not call so late.

Poor ANDY sits in a hypnotic trance
Thralled by a psycho-medical romance

Dealing with Brokers, Cancers, Sexual Force—
In which REEVES is the Superman, of course.
We sneer, and sit, and fall beneath the spell,—
And Time stands still,—and we are thralled as well;
The charm is smashed; we hint "The hour is late"—
But REEVES continues boldly to narrate.
ROG suddenly remembers there is due
At nine A.M. an article or two,
And for his typewriter he makes a break;
For there's a spicy interview to fake,
Dramatic dope, some fourteen thousand words,—
And verse, to fill a column and two thirds.
Slyly and quickly we become undressed—
Slyly and silently we seek the nest.
I doze; but hear, ere yet oblivion
Enfolds,—REEVES lecturing the rising sun,
And ROGERS, plangent on His Remington.

A Farmer's Woman

I know a patient, nobly-curving hill
That wears a different paleness every hour,—
Copper by sun-grey-velvet through a shower,—
Topaz and mauve,—blue of the heron's quill,
Forever mean-souled ploughmen scar the soil,
And bind, with rambling stony walls, her breast—
Never allow her weary womb to rest,
Nor give a moment's peace for all her toil.

O, if the ploughman knew what wonders spring
From fields that for a season fallow lie—
Under the healing hand of wind and sky—
Would they not grant her time for flowering!
Her heart is rock. I wonder if her tongue
Knows how to say "I also once was young?"

The Great Adventure

(A Rhymed Review)

If I were England's greatest painter
    (Let's say, the William Chase of Britain),
Living alone—and what is quainter,
    Cursed with the shyness of a kitten—
    (For so has Arnold Bennett written.)

And if my valet up and died,
    Would I be so abjectly flabby
As under his name try and hide,
    While he is buried in the Abbey?
    (Who knows? Qui sait? Wer kennt? Quien sabe?)

I know men who, to sell a picture,
    Would place themselves in that position.
How much less, then is this a stricture!
    The Abbey is the proud ambition
    Of every Royal Academician!

I might do this, I might do that;
    Apocryphal as is the plot, sir,
But as for living in a flat
    In Putney, I would rather not, sir—
    Two years? I'd sooner far be shot, sir!

About this here artistic shyness:
    I've not seen Sargent blush and stutter,
Or Borglum sneak around with slyness,
    Or Kenyon Cox grow white and flutter—
    (But then they must make bread and butter!)

And yet, we should of course remember
    It's all O.K. in the the-ay-tre;
And if this show runs till December
    'Twill indicate that it doth pay ter
    Bedramatrize a second-rater!

Love at Sea

Wind smothers the snarling of the great ships,
And the serene gulls are stronger than turbines;
Mile upon mile the hiss of a stumbling wave breaks unbroken—
Yet stronger is the power of your lips for my lips.

This cool green fluid death shall toss us living
Higher than high heaven and deeper than sighs—
But O the abrupt, stiff, sloping, resistless foam
Shall not forbid our taking and our giving!

Life wrenched from its roots—what wretchedness!
What waving of lost tentacles like blind sea-things!
Even the still ooze beneath is quick and profound—
I am less and more than I was, you are more and less.

I cried upon God last night, and God was not where I cried;
He was slipping and balancing on the thoughtless shifting
    planes of sea.
Careless and cruel, he will unchain the appalling sea-gray
    engines—
But the speech of your body to my body will not be denied!

Florence

Summer of 1913

Make way for him, Giotto, Dante, Bianco Capello,
And all the glories of an ancient anarchy,—
Make way, loud Byron, sinning by the rule of three,
For this becivilized, berouged, befinished fellow,—
Collector of green jade fruits, and amateur of yellow;
Even beside the Uffizzi and the Bargello

He looks incredibly mean!
Make way, dead giant Italy, for Robert de la Condamine!

O Heir of all the Ages! Why should they have an heir?
There is no legacy but ashes of old fiery Te Deums
Neatly arranged in libraries and museums.
So he can languidly sniff their immortal essence there!
Distill from their fury an oil to anoint his hair!
From their violence, strength for a minor poet's dare!
The Superman has mastered his own soul—
Now less than these, who theirs could not control!

Here the air is choked with the crowding-up, struggling
    souls of the dead—
Here death is swifter than life, and the green sky spawns
    no bursting stars—
The peasants sing old songs, and sleep with their avatars,—
And the strong, heady tongue that was born of lawlessness,
    is talking law instead.
O Field of Dragons' Teeth, where turbulent armies bred,
Horrors and heroes the fruit of one monstrous marriage bed,
Miraculous Tuscan soil
That now breeds only the seasons, olive and wine, wine and oil!

Here where the olden poets came in beauty to die
I sit in a walled high garden, far from the sound of change,
Watching the great clouds boil up from the Vallombrosa range
And sunlight pour through the black cypresses, drenching the
    Vineyards dry.
Here is the drunken peace of the sensuous sick,—and
    here am I,
Smelling the smoke from clanging cities, that hangs like
    a threat in the sky
Unknown to these clods
Who worship Bacchus and Pan, and the senile young gods!

Through the halls of the Medici, queenlier far than they,
Walks she I love, half peasant, half courtesan,—
In her right hand a man's death, in her left the life of a man,—
Beware which you choose, for she changes them day by day;

Sun and wind in the room of her soul, and all the beasts
    that prey!
O let us shake off this smothering silky death, let us go away,
My dearest old dear
Mabel! What are we living things doing here?

The Exile

(Translated from a Mexican Ballad)

I wandered out an exile through the world,
    Ostracized by the government.
I came back in a year
    With the fondness of love.
I went away with the purpose
    Of being able to remain abroad
And the love for that woman was the only thing
    That made me come back.

Oh what cheerless nights I spent,
    Such nights without you, my life.
Not one relative, not one friend,
    To whom I may murmur my sorrows.
I went with the only purpose
    Of remaining away from my country,
And the love of that woman was the only thing
    That ever brought me back.

Feigned

(Translated from a Mexican Ballad)

If it is a fault to love you so,
And if my weeping can move you any,
If you do not believe nor love me

Why do you listen to me; why do you call me?

If my pleadings do not move you
If you draw away when I come near,
If you never sigh when you see me,
Why do you call me, why do you regard me?

Oh constant longing,
Soul of my soul,
Life of my happiness
Give me disappointment,
But don't leave me in doubt.

Because when you depart from my sight
You renew my longings,
Tormenting my life,
Feigning anger, which is pain,
For a love that is hidden,
And an obstinate blushing—
That which you call oblivion,
Is what is called love.

Morning Song to Gen. Francisco Villa And to his Leaders and Officers on their Arrival at Torreon

(Translated from a Mexican Ballad)

Here is Francisco Villa
With his leaders and his officers
Who came to saddle the shortys
Of the old Federal Army.

Here is a famous General,
Of great courage and reliable,
And Mr. V. Carranza,
Has placed his eyes upon him.

Get ready now Red Flaggers,
Who have been talking so loud,
Because Villa and his soldiers,
Will soon set you straight.

His soldiers are not "runners,"
Nor do they fear the cannon.
They relied on their manhood,
and took Torreon.

Now Shortys of the Bravo
Now that you are in your hole,
Your father, Monclovio Herrera,
Will surely cut your tail.

Today has come your tamer,
The father of Rooster trainers,
To run you away from Torreon,
To the Devil with all your hides,

On this day the Gachupines,
As things went all against them,
Their fortresses were as nothing
And as nothing their "Social Defense."

The rich with plenty of money
Have already got their whipping,
As the soldiers of Urbina
Know, and those of Monclovio Herrera.

Fly, fly away, little dove,
And go through all the meadows,
And announce the arrival of Villa
To drive them all out forever.

This is the end of ambition,
And justice will be the winner,
For Villa has reached Torreon,
To punish the avaricious.

Bravo has always dreamed,

That he would triumph promptly
Here he saw the apparition
Of Juan Diego in Pancho Villa.

The great "Defensa Social"
Made up of the Four Hundred,
All intended to maltreat us,
As if we were their donkeys.

But the people who have confidence
And never lose their hopes,
Have relied with much faith
On the forces of Carranza.

There came Villa, the fighter,
With his insurgent army,
Fighting with great valor,
To avenge Madero.

The people are all with him
And also show him honor,
For they trust he will vanquish
Every one of the traitors.

Fly away our Royal Eagle,
These laurels bear to Villa,
For he has come to conquer
Bravo and all his leaders.

Now, ye sons of the mosquito,
Your pride will come to an end,
If Villa has come here
It is because he could do it.

Villa came with his cannons,
To spoil the bad combination
And now Bravo and his Baldys,
Soon "took a hike."

On hearing him mentioned,
As a famous General,
They run to seek a shelter

In quarters unmentioned.

The rich who talked so much
Have had their whipping.
They said they nothing feared,
But now have got what was coming.

Viva Villa and his soldiers!
Viva Herrera and his people!
You have seen, wicked people,
What the brave man can do.

They struggle for the right
They struggle for equality,
They struggle for our liberty
And struggle for our Nation.

Fly away, little dove,
And take this charm with you.
Go ask them in Torreon,
How did they fare with Villa.

He came from Chihuahua,
And came to give them a shaking,
But arriving in Torreon,
He found how the tide was turning.

That in spite of a thousand fortresses,
He came to take the city;
Just to put an end to Bravo,
And all his fancy puppets.

All those who maltreat the poor,
And now are planning his ruin,
In the end will not escape,
For they will go through the machine.

Poor Baldys of today,
And also the Red-Flaggers!
For Villa with his cannons
Has given them indigestion.

Fly, fly away, little dove,

And stop in the gardens,
For Villa arrives today,
Marching through the country.

Many have run away,
Trying to save themselves,
But already they are pursued,
And perhaps will not escape.

With this now I say goodby,
By the rose of Castile.
Here is the end of my rhyme,
To the great General Villa.

Winter Night

High hands the hollow, ringing shield of heaven,
Embossed with stars. The thin air wounds like steel,
Stark and resilient as a Spanish blade.
Sharp snaps the rigid lake's mysterious ice,
And the prim, starchy twigs of naked trees
Crackle metallic in an unfelt wind.
A light-poised Damoclean scimitar
The faintly-damascened pale moon. Benumbed
Shrinks the racked earth gripped in the hand of Cold.
O hark! Swift, anvil-ringing iron hoofs
Drum down the boreal interstellar space;
The Blue Knight rides, spurring his snorting stallion
Out of the dark side of the frozen moon—
Eyes crueller than a beryl-sheathed crevasse,
Breath like the chilly fog of polar seas,
Glaciers for armor on his breast and thighs,
A polished Alp for helmet, and for plume
The league-long Northern Lights behind him floating.
Wave on wave of prismatic blazoning,

Glorious up the sky!
                    The Blue Knight rides
With his moon-shimmering, star-tipped lance at rest,—
Drives at the world—Crash! and the brittle globe
Bursts like a crystal goblet,—shivering, falling,—
Shivers, splinters brustling, tinkling, jarring,
Jingling in fading dissonance down the void—
Jangling down the unplumbed void forever. . . .

Winter: A Fragment

On the south side of the hill
Out of the wind
I sat me down to rest.
At my back a lichened wall,
A rough, heaped-up wall of grey boulders,—
(What patient labor of men goes into the gathering of stones!)
Under my feet the rusty fields—
Brush of smoke-rose, yellow reeds, dull purple masses of
    trees fretting the pale sky,
A world cleft in irregular blocks of ashen colors
By blundering stone-walls that cast black shadows.
Over against me a hill crouched in desolation like a lion;
A jade-colored rock upon his breast
Fountained a living spring,
Frozen in monstrous shapes, a row of alabaster gods
Grotesque, with hands upon their knees
Like Hindu idols guarding a king's tomb
And O, the subtle-toned and bristling marsh
Dead-rose and olive-green, white shields of ice beneath—
Russet and amber and faded lilac,—dimmed like breath
    on a mirror
Blended and toned as colors seen through a fog,—
Yet under the cold thin light of the wintry day
Fixed, bloodless and dead.

So, gazing upon last year's furrows, and the marks of
    old ploughs,
And the drear scattered houses, feathered with little
    smoke,
And the lean cattle backing to the wind,
And the dun hobbling men stiffly carrying in wood,
And the pale thwarted faces of their women at the
    windows,—
I thought this is death,—this is lassitude and
    sterility, unending,—
Rock and weeds and back-bowing work have stunted the
    soul of this place,
Faith has the world none, nor future save fruitless,
    monotonous drudgery,—
Stunted souls too weary to aspire,—and deadened
    brains too driven to do better.
Anemic fields unfertile with much ploughing.

Fog

Death comes like this, I know—
Snow-soft and gently cold;
Impalpable battalion of thin mist,
Light-quenching and sound-smothering and slow.

Black as a wind-spilled sail
The spent world flaps in space—
Day's but a grayer night, and the old sun
Up the blind sky goes heavily and pale.

Out of all circumstance
I drift or seem to drift
In a vague vapor-world that clings and veils
Great trees a row like kneeling elephants.

How vast your voice is grown
That was so silver-soft;
Dim dies the candle-glory of your face—
Though we go hand in hand, I am alone.

Now love and all the warm
Pageant of livingness
Trouble my quiet like forgotten dreams
Of ancient thunder on the hills of storm

Aforetime I have kissed
The feet of many gods;
But in this empty place there is no God
Save only I, a naked egoist.

How loud, how terribly
Aflame are lights and sounds!
And yet I know beyond the fog is naught
But lonely bells across gray wastes of sea . . .

Pygmalion

Pygmalion, Pygmalion, Pygmalion—
A mountain meadow loved Pygmalion.
Where a great shining rock like a fallen shield
Lay heavily in tall grass, he rested once.
Long did it hold the pulsing warmth of his body.
And the apple-tree that shaded him, remembered him;
Grass that was new-born trembled under his feet—
Old withered grass felt green beneath his feet—
And the wide view that sank like sleep after pain
Miles over toppling hills to the wide, still river,
Robed itself in opal, golden and haze for him.

While the sun's shadow stood between light and light
He came, paused, and was gone. Though never, never
In the world's old contentment had there passed
Before him any human in this place,
Yet lonely were the rock, the tree, the grass.
Longing of the starved heart for a lover gone,
When all is as before, and yet how empty!

White moved his body, crushing the ferns in the valley,
And his happy singing died along far roads;

But love followed after him—flickered across his sleep,
Breathed pride into his walk, power into his hand,
Sweet restlessness into his quiet thought—
Till he who had needed life now needed more;
And so at last he came to the hills again.

Pygmalion, Pygmalion, Pygmalion—
He said in his pride "Thou art wild, and without life!"
Never feeling the warm dispersed quiet of earth,
Or the slow stupendous heart-beat that hills have.

Pygmalion, Pygmalion, Pygmalion—
He wrenched the shining rock from the meadow's breast,
And out of it shaped the lovely, almost-breathing
Form of his dream of his love of the world's women.
Slim and white was she, whimsical, full of caprice;
Bright sharp in sunlight, languid in shadow of cloud,
Pale in the dawn, and flushed at the end of day.
Staring, he felt of a sudden the quick, fierce urge
Of the will of the grass, and the rock, and the flowering
     tree;
Knew himself weak and unfulfilled without her—
Knew that he bore his own doom in his breast—
Slave of a stone, unmoving, cold to his touch,
Loving in a stone's way, loving but thrilling never.

In smothering summer silence, pricked with crickets,
Still fell the smiting hammer; happy and loud
Swelled the full-throated song of the adult grass . . .
Full-breasted dropped the tree, heavy with apples . . .
A wind worn lean from leap-frog over the mountains
Spurted the stiff faun-hair of him—whipped desire,
And a bird sang "Faint-faint-faint with love-love-love!"

Blind he stood, while the great sun blundered down
Through planets strung like beads on careless orbits;
Blind to the view that sank like sleep after love,
Miles over blasoned hills to the brazen river,
Ceaselessly changing, color and form and line,
Pomp, glaze, pageantry new to the world's delight . . .

Hot moist hands on the glittering flanks, and eager
Hands following the chill hips, the icy breasts—
Lithe, radiant, belly to swelling stone—
"Galatea!"—blast of whispering flame his throat—
"Galatea! Galatea!"—his entrails molten fire—
"Galatea Galatea! Galatea!" mouth to mouth . . .

Light shadows of driven clouds on a summer lake—
Ripples on still ponds, winds that ruffle and pass—
Happy young grass rising to drink the rain—
So Galatea under his kisses stirred;
Like a white moth alighted breath on her lips,
Like a blue rent in a storm-sky opened her eyes.
Sweetly the new blood leaped and sang in her veins,
Dumbly, blindly her hands, breast, mouth sought his . .

Pygmalion, Pygmalion, Pygmalion—
Rock is she still, and her heart is the hill's heart,
Full of all things beside him—full of wind and bees
And the long falling miles and miles of air.
Despair and gnawing are on him, and he knows her
Unattainable who is born of will and hill—
Far-bright as a plunging full-sailed ship that seems
Hull-down to be set immutable in sea. . . . . .

A Dedication

To Max Eastman

There was a man, who, loving quiet beauty best
Yet could not rest.
Attuned to the majestic rhythm of whirling suns
That chimes and runs
Through happy stillnesses—birth in the dawn, and stark
Love in the dark;
The unconquerable semen of the world, that mounts
    and sings
Through endless springs,

101

And the dumb death-like sleep of the winter-withered hill
That warms life still;
There was a man, who, loving quiet beauty best,
Yet could not rest
For the harsh moaning of unhappy humankind,
Fettered and blind—
Too driven to know beauty and too hungry-tired
To be inspired.
From his high-windy-peaceful hill, he stumbled down
Into the town,
With a child's eyes, clear bitterness, and silver scorn
Of the outworn
And cruel mastery of life by senile death;
And with his breath
Fanned up the noble fires that smoulder in the breast
Of the oppressed.
What guerdon, to forswear for dust and some and this
The high-souled bliss
Of poets in walled gardens, finely growing old,
Serene and cold?
A vision of new splendor in the human scheme—
A god-like dream—
And a new lilt of happy trumpets in the strange
Clangor of Change!

Hospital Notes

Coming out of Ether.

Swish—swish—flash by the spokes of the Wheel of Pain;
Dissily runs the whining rim.
Way down in the cool dark is slow-revolving sleep,
But I hang heavily writhing in hot chains
High in the crimson stillness of my body,
And the swish-swish of the spokes of the Wheel of Pain.

Clinic

Square white cells, all in a row, with ground-glass windows;
Tubes treasuring sacraments of suffering, rubber pipes,
    apparatus;
Walls maculate with old yellow and brown. . . .
Out of a mass of human flesh, hairy and dull,
Slim shining steel grows, dripping slow pale thick drops,
And regularly, like distant whistles in a fog, groaning. . . .
Young interns, following the great surgeon like chicks a hen,
Crowd in as he pokes, wrenches, and dictates over his shoulder,
And hurries on, deaf to the shuddering spirit, rapt in a
    dream of machinery.

Operating Room

Sunlight floods the shiny many-windowed place.
Coldly glinting on flawless steel under glass,
And blaring imperially on the spattered gules,
Where kneeling men grunt as they swab the floor.
Startled eyes of nurses swish by noiselessly,
Orderlies with cropped heads swagger like murderers;
And three surgeons, robed and masked mysteriously,
Lounge gossiping of guts, and wish it were lunch-time.
Beyond the porcelain door, screaming mounts crescendo—
Case 4001 coming out of the ether,
Born again half a man, to spend his life in bed.

Two Rooms

"And I will make a song for the ears of the President,
    full of weapons and menacing points,
"And behind the weapons countless dissatisfied faces."
                    —Walt Whitman, "Leaves of Grass," 1867
                    60
"Suite number 60 consists of an extra large room on the
    quiet side of the building, with private bath and extra
    service. The rate is $15 per day."
                    —Hospital Catalogue.

103

There was a bustle in the ward the day he came,
A smell of cold furs, purr of limousines,
A sharp-heeled chauffeur carrying valises
And staggering flunkey feet supporting him.

The nurse was excited. "Who d'you think's in 60?
"Bertram C. Pick, you know, the Ice Trust man.
"My, you just ought to see his overcoat—
"Real sable. And the Mayor sent some orchids. . . .
"One of the girls went in to see if he wanted anything,
"And he just opened his eyes and swore at her. . . .
"His night nurse is a friend of mine, Belle Stevens
"Her name is; she says he's as democratic
"As if he didn't have ten million dollars. . . ."

"Bright's," my doctor told me, looking serious.
"Too much drink, strong cigars—er—no exercise,
"The cares and responsibilities of a great corporation . . .
"A big man, splendid advertising for the hospital—
"Not much hope—too bad—a loss to the country. . . ."
There were two world-known specialists in attendance—
One cabled for across three thousand sea-miles—
The house-physician and two jealous interns,
They gave out hourly bulletins to the papers,
And three reporters camped out in the waiting-room . . .

The orderly was aglow with reflected greatness.
"All swelled-up and yellow-faced he lies there,
"A short fat man, rolling around and grunting.
"The head-nurse says, 'Would you like a private nurse, sir?
" 'Thirty dollars a week—' And he breaks in,
" 'Gimme a couple. I don't care what they cost!'
"Like it was nothing. The paper says he's got
"A steam yacht, private car, and he don't know how many
        automobiles;
"A house in New York, and places in Newport and Florida . . .
"Well, one thing's sure, he can't take 'em with him
"Where he's going. But if *I* had 'em, *I* should worry!"

The last few days his wife and daughter sat
Rustling silks and whispering, outside my door . . .
"Why can't I?" hissed a hard, querulous young voice,
"The Bevins went abroad when Jasper died,
"And nobody thought anything about it—
"I'm sick of staying around here all my life
"Without enough money to do what I please;
"I'm going to travel now and have some fun!"

Toward the end, as he twisted gasping on his bed
In that quiet room, with his special nurses and orderlies,
And all that science can do, to ease his body,
And orchids to ease his soul, and telegrams and cables
From kings, presidents, parliaments, stock-exchanges
I wonder if his burning kidney reminded him
Of that hot summer, when the fevered slums
Spewed out dead babies, and he made his pile . . .

53

"Rooms 53 and 54 are furnished and endowed by Mrs.
Bertram C. Pick, in memory of her husband. They can be had
for the minimum rate of $4 per day, payable in advance."
                                        —Hospital Catalogue.

I knew him only by his ludicrous screaming—
Four times a day, three times a night—
Before they punched him with the hypodermic.
"O my God, I can't stand it! O my God, give me something!"
And then the nurse came grumbling in
Scolding, "You ought to be ashamed of yourself—"
And the bitter morphine dragged his yelling down
Dissonantly to a groan, a mumble.—

The Doctor said,
"A most interesting case.
"An acute cystitis, long neglected,

"Infected bladder, ureters, kidneys,—in fact
"The entire superpubic—you wouldn't understand.
"Possibly a year's rest in a warm climate
"Might have cleared up all the symptoms.
"Yes, now there's nothing to be done
"But morphine injections to dull the pain . . .
"How long? O consciousness will probably
"Persist six weeks—and by that time the sedative
"Will be powerless; and then two weeks coma. . . .
"It is extraordinarily virulent. I've never seen
"Such rapid progress. . . . Kill him? Ha, ha.
"Well no, really. It's our duty, you know,
"To preserve life as long as possible—and besides,
"The last stages are particularly interesting. . . ."

The nurse said,
"These kind of patients are a bother.
"They make so much noise nobody else can sleep,
"And the whole ward's got to tend to them.
"A man as sick as that ought to have a private nurse;
"Well, if he can't afford it, he oughtn't to be here
"Spending four dollars a day. There's the public ward,
"That's free, and as good a place to die as this . . ."
"Yes, a wife. She was here at first,
"Found out how long it would last, and paid
"Five weeks in advance. Said she couldn't stay
"But had to go home and work for the rest
"Before it was due. That's what I call funny!"

The orderly said,
"He puts his finger on the bell
"And keeps it there; and if I don't come he hollers.
"Last time I got mad. 'What in hell,' I says
" 'Do you think I am? Your private valley?' I says . . .
"When he come here he had on overalls,
"A brick-layer, I think he was—can't even talk
"Good grammar . . . Say, you ought to see him stripped;
"Legs like tooth-picks, and the comicalest thin tail . . .

106

"Say, you know why he don't take no baths?
"Because we're scared he'll go down through the plug-hole
"And stop up the pipes—pretty good, eh?"

Well, he staid in 53—so his wife was working.
And before the dope stopped acting, he was so weak
You could hardly hear his wheezing moan at all,
Although you knew his soul was screaming always . . .
And then even that stopped, and the nurse sighed
Relievedly. "Thank heavens,' she said, "That's over . . .
"Did you hear us girls all laughing this morning?
"The new patient in 45—he's the funniest man
"I ever heard talk. The first thing he says to me,
"When I put the thermometer into his mouth, was,
" 'Don't you go off to the movies now!' "

But all I could think of was death in 53
Without love, or battle, or any glorious suddenness . . .

On Returning To The City

(An unpublished fragment)

Last night I could not sleep for longing—
Despite the wind-rush of the rain,
The breathless engine-bell's ding-donging,
And the smooth roaring of the train . . .

A blur of light—an echoing thunder—
The little towns sprang up—were gone—
Then leaped my soul and I asunder,
And the impetuous soul rushed on

To greet those towers where the morning
First flashes from the rim of sea,
Last pinnacles of sun's adorning—
Manhattan! Breath and blood of me!

Manhattan, zoned with ships, and cruel

107

Youngest of all the world's great towns;
Her bodice quick with many a jewel,
Imperially crowned with crowns—

Manhattan, menacing above her
The dull gods gaping in the sky—
A Titaness without a lover,
Ringed with a million such as I,

Who burn with an impassioned gladness
To price what never has been priced—
To sting her sullen blood to madness
And fill her with a strong-armed Christ.

The word! The Word that has no naming,—
Tuned to her mighty pulses' beat,—
That shall awake her senses flaming,
Reckless, and terrible, and sweet.

Then shall burst from her lips such singing
As the gods heard at Baldur's birth—
And all her garments from her flinging,
White, naked, she shall stun the earth!

America 1918

Across the sea my country, my America,
Girt with steel, hard-glittering with power,
As a champion, with great voice trumpeting
High words, "For Liberty . . . Democracy . . ."

Deep within me something stirs, answers—
(My country, my America!)
As if alone in the high and empty night
She called me—my lost one, my first lover
I love no more, love no more, love no more . . .
The cloudy shadow of old tenderness,
Illusions of beautiful madness—many deaths
And easy immortality . . .

I

By my free boyhood in the wide West,
The powerful sweet river, fish-wheels, log-rafts,
Ships from behind the sunset, Lascar-manned,
Chinatown, throbbing with mysterious gongs,
The blue thunderous Pacific, blaring sunsets,
Black smoking forests on surf-beaten headlands,
Lost beaches, camp-fires, wail of hunting cougars . . .
By the rolling range, and the flat sun-smitten desert,
Night with coyotes yapping, domed with burst of stars,
The grey herd moving eastward, towering dust,
Ropes whistling in slow coils, hats flapping, yells . . .
By miles of yellow wheat rippling in the Chinook,
Orchards forever endless, deep in blooming,
Green-golden orangegroves and snow-peaks looming over .
By raw audacious cities sprung from nothing,
Brawling and bragging in their careless youth . . .
I know thee, America!

Fishermen putting out from Astoria in the foggy dawn
        their double-bowed boats,
Lean cow-punchers jogging south from Burns, with faces
        burned leathery and silent,
Stringy old prospectors trudging behind reluctant pack-
        horses, across the Nevada alkali,
Hunters coming out of the brush at night-fall on the
        brink of the Lewis and Clark canyon,
Grunting as they slide off their fifty-pound packs and
        look around for a place to make camp,
Forest rangers standing on a bald peak and sweeping
        the wilderness for smoke,
Big-gloved brakemen walking the top of a swaying freight,
        spanner in hand, biting off a hunk of plug,
Lumbermen with spiked boots and timber-hook, riding
        the broken jam in white water,
Indians on the street-corner in Pocatello, pulling out
        chin-whiskers with a pair of tweezers and a pocket-
        mirror,

Or down on the Siuslaw, squatting behind their summer
    lodges listening to Caruso on a two-hundred-dollar
    phonograph,
Loud-roaring Alaska miners, smashing looking-glasses,
    throwing the waiter a five-dollar gold-piece for a
    shot of whiskey and telling him to keep the change,
Keepers of dance-halls in construction camps, bar-keeps,
    prostitutes,
Bums riding the rods, wobblies singing their defiant,
    songs, unafraid of death,
Card-sharps and real-estate agents, timber-kings,
    wheat-kings, cattle-kings . . .
I know ye, Americans!

2.

By my bright youth in golden eastern towns . . .

Harvard . . . pain of growing, ecstasy of unfolding,
Thrill of books, thrill of friendship, hero-worship,
Intoxication of dancing, tempest of great music,
Squandering delight, first consciousness of power . . .
Wild nights in Boston, battles with policemen,
Picking up girls, nights of lurid adventure . . .
Winter swims at L Street, breaking the ice
Just for the strong shock on a hard body . . .
And the huge Stadium heaving up its thousands
With cadenced roaring cheer or song tremendous
When Harvard scored on Yale . . . By this, by this
I know thee, America!

By proud New York and its man-piled Matterhorns,
The hard blue sky overhead and the west wind blowing,
Steamplumes waving from sun-glittering pinnacles,
And deep streets shaking to the million-river—

> *Manhattan, zoned with ships, the cruel*
> *Youngest of all the world's great towns,*
> *Thy bodice bright with many a jewel,*
> *Imperially crowned with crowns . . .*

Who that hath known thee but shall burn
In exile till he come again
To do thy bitter will, O stern
Moon of the tides of men!

Soaring Fifth Avenue, Peacock Street, Street of banners,
Ever-changing pageant of splendid courtesans,
Fantastic color, sheen of silks and silver, toy-dogs,
Procession of automobiles like jewel-boxes—
Traffic-cop majestical with lifted yellow hand—
Palaces, hotels gigantic, old men in club-windows,
Sweat-shops belching their dun armies at noon-time,
Parades, mile-waves of uniforms flowing up
Bands crashing, between the black still masses of people . . .

Broadway, gashing the city like a lava-stream,
Crowned with shower of sparks, as a beaten fire,
Blazing theatres, brazen restaurants, smell of talc,
Movie mansions, hock-shops, imitation diamonds,
Chorus-girls making the rounds of the booking-agencies,
Music-factories blatting from twenty-five pianos,
And all the hectic world of paint and shirt-front . . .

Old Greenwich Village, citadel of amateurs,
Battle-ground of all adolescent Utopias,
Half sham-Bohemia, dear to uptown slummers,
Half sanctuary of the outcast and dissatisfied . . .
Free fellowship of painters, sailors, poets,
Light women, Uranians, tramps, and strike-leaders,
Actresses, models, people with aliases or nameless,
Sculptors who run elevators for a living,
Musicians who have to pound pianos in picture-houses . . .
Workers, dissipating, most of them young, most of them poor,
Playing at art, playing at love, playing at rebellion,
In the enchanted borders of the impossible republic . . .

Mysteriously has word of it gone forth
To lonely cabins in the Virginia mountains,
Logging-camps in the Maine woods, desert ranches,

111

Farms lost in vastnesses of Dakota wheat . . .
Wherever young heart-hungry dreamers of splendor
Can find in all the hard immensity of America
No place to fashion beauty, no companion
To shameless talk of loveliness and love,
Here would they be, elbow on a wooden table at Polly's,
Or, borrowing a fiver, over Burgundy at the Brevoort,
Arguing about Life, and Sex, and the Revolution . . .

The East Side, worlds within a world, chaos of nations,
Sink of the nomad races, last and wretchedest
Port of the westward Odyssey of mankind . . .
At dawn vomiting colossal flood of machine-fodder,
At evening sucking back with terrible harsh sound
To beast-like tenements, garish nickelodeons, gin-mills . . .
Kids hanging round the corner saloon, inhaling cheap cigarettes,
Leering at the short-skirted girls who two by two go giggling by
Picking their way between crawling babies, over the filthy
    sidewalk . . .
Children at shrill daring games under the hoofs of truck-
    horses—
Gaunt women screaming at them and each other, in twanging
    foreign tongues—
Old men sitting on the crowded stoop in shirt-sleeves,
    smoking an evening pipe,
Glare of push-cart torches ringer with alien faces . . .

In dim Rumanian wine-cellars I am not unwelcome,
Pulsing with hot rhythm of scornful gypsy fiddlers . . .
In Grand Street coffee-rooms, haunt of Yiddish philosophers,
Novelists reading aloud a new chapter, collecting a dime
    from each auditor,
Playwrights dramatizing the newspaper headlines, poets
    dumb to deaf America . . .
Fenian saloons, with prominent green flag, and a framed
    bond of the Irish Republic over the bar,
Italian *ristorantes,* Chianti and spontaneous tenors,
Armenian kitchens hung with Oriental carpets from New Jersey,

112

Where hawk-faced men whisper over thick coffee, fingering
   tesbiehs . . .
German *bier-stuben,* painted with fat mottoes . . . French
   cafes, neat madame at the *caisse,*
Greek *kaffeinias,* chop-suey joints with contemptuous
   slant-eyed waiters . . .
Theatres, Italian marionettes gesticulating Tasso
Flabby burlesque at Miner's . . . Tomashevsky's Jewish
   coryphees,
Offenbach in Irving Place winey sap and sparkle,
La Scala Opera Company in "Otello" at the Verdi—
Ragged costumes, toppling scenery, and voices glorious . . .
And the Sicilian Duse, glowing through Giovanitti's
   Tenebri Rossi
Like a volcanic daybreak over the Siberian tundra . . .

Well do I know the Russian brass-shops on Allen Street,
The opium-stinking dens of the Cantonese lottery-men,
And where the Syrians sell their cool grey water-jars . . .
Chatham Square, framed in monstrous kinema-signs and the
   saloons of the damned.
Bowery old-clothes men, stale and sand-floored drinking-rooms,
   spotted with old spittle,
Beef-steak John's, spoke of by sailors in the uttermost ports
   of earth,
Peter Cooper Square in the sick light of before-dawn
Heaped up with homeless men . . . the ten-cent lodging houses
Where shaking wrecks sit dully picking lice around the
   red-hot stove . . .
Stuss-games in sinister back-rooms over on Avenue A,
Dingy law-offices in the shadow of the Tombs, shrines of
   unclean miracles,
The blasted twilight under the hysterical thunder of the
   East River bridges,
And South Street fragrant still with spices of long-
   vanished clipper-ships . . .

Dear and familiar and unforgettable is the city
As the face of my mother . . .

City Hall, never-still whirlpool of the seven millions,
Drowned in the crashing ebb and flow of Brooklyn Bridge,
Human cascades from the Elevated, and the Subway geysers
    spouting . . .
Tall humming newspaper-offices aglitter till the dawn,
Flocks of little newsboys like dusty sparrows
Splashing in the forbidden fountains . . . sleeping bums . . .
In the far-flung shadow of legendary towers . . .
The Battery, sea-wind cool, at the foot of the sky-
    scraper precipice,
And the sonorous great ships going by, bound for the
    ends of sea,
Squat hurtling ferries, barges stiff with box-cars,
    eagle-crested tugs,
Yellow spray leaping the sea-wall, hoarse gulls
    circling over,
And Liberty lifting gigantic, menacing, out of the
    strife of keels,
Behind it crouching Ellis Island, purgatory of freedom . . .

Exotic negro-town, upper Amsterdam Avenue,
And its black sensuous easily-happy people, shunned of men,
The Dark-town Follies, and Europe's ragtime orchestra . . .
Central Park, elegant motors purring along the drive,
Smart cavaliers, perambulators of the upper-classes,
Lovers on benches uneasily spooning, one eye out for the cops
And the gasping slums poured out hot summer nights to sleep
    on the meadows . . .
Harlem, New York second-hand and slightly cheaper,
Bronx, post-graduate ghetto, scabby growth of new tenements,
Vast green-glowing parks, and the frayed edge of the country . . .

Have I omitted you, truck-quaking West Street, dingy
    Death Avenue,
Gracious old Church of the Sea and Land, Inwood, tip of
    Manhattan,
The rag-shops of Minetta Lane, and the yelping swirl of
    the Broad Street Curb,
Macdougal Alley, gilded squalor of fashionable artists,

Coenties Slip, old sea-remembering notch at the back of
     down-town—?
May, across the world, three thousand miles away, without
     map or guide-book,
Ask me and I will describe them, and their people,
In all weathers, drunk or sober, by sun and moon . . .

I have watched the summer day come up from the top of
     a pier of the Williamsburgh Bridge,
I have slept in a basket of squid at the Fulton Street
     Market,
Talked about God with the old cockney woman who sells
     hot-dogs under the Elevated at South Ferry,
Listened to tales of dago dips in the family parlor of
     the Hell-hole,
And from the top gallery of the Metropolitan heard Didur
     sing "Boris Godounov". . .
I have shot craps with gangsters in the Gas House district,
And seen what happens to a green bull on San Juan Hill . . .
I can tell you where to hire a gunman to croak a squealer,
And where young girls are bought and sold, and how to get
     coke on 125th Street
And what men talk about behind Steve Brodie's, or in the
     private rooms of the Lafayette Baths . . .
Dear and familiar and ever-new to me is the city
As the body of my lover . . .
All sounds—harsh clatter of the Elevated, rumble of
     the Subway,
Tapping of policemen's clubs on midnight pavements,
Hand-organs plaintive and monotonous, squawking motor-
     horns,
Gatling crepitation of airy riveters,
Muffled detonations deep down underground,
Flat bawling of newsboys, quick-clamoring ambulance gongs,
Deep nervous tooting from the evening harbor,
And the profound shuffling thunder of myriad feet . . .

All smells—smell of sample shoes, second-hand clothing,
Dutch bakeries, Sunday delicatessen, kosher cooking,
Smell of damp tons of newspapers along Park Row,

115

The Subway, smelling like the tomb of Rameses the Great,
The tired odor of infinite human dust, drug-stores,
And the sour slum stench of mean streets . . .
People—rock-eyed brokers gambling with Empires,
Swarthy insolent boot-blacks, cringing push-cart peddlers,
The white-capped wop flipping wheat-cakes in the window
    of Childs',
Sallow-garment-workers coughing on a park-bench in the
    thin spring sun,
Dully watching the leaping fountain as they eat a hand-
    ful of peanuts for lunch . . .
The steeple-jack swaying infinitesimal at the top of the
    Woodworth flag-pole,
Charity workers driving hard bargains for the degrada-
    tion of the poor,
Worn-out snarling street-car conductors, sentimental
    prize-fighters,
White-wings scouring the roaring traffic-ways, foul-
    mouthed truck-drivers,
Spanish longshoremen heaving up freight-mountains,
    hollow-eyed silk-weavers,
Structural steel workers catching hot rivets on high-up
    spidery girders,
Sand-hogs in hissing air-locks under the North River,
    sweating Subway muckers, hard-rock men blasting
    beneath Broadway,
Ward-leaders with uptilted cigars, planning mysterious
    underground battles for power,
Raucous soap-boxers in Union Square, preaching the ever-
    lasting crusade,
Pale half-fed cash-girls in department stores, gaunt
    children making paper-flowers in dim garrets,
Princess stenographers, and manicures chewing gum with
    a queenly air,
Macs, whore-house madams, street-walkers, touts, bouncers,
    stool-pigeons . . .
All professions, races, temperaments, philosophies,
All history, all possibilities, all romance,
America . . . the world . . . !

A Letter to Louise*

Rainy rush of bird-song
Apple-blossom smoke
Thin bells water-falling sound
Wind-rust on the silver pond
Furry starring willow-wand
Wan new grasses waking round
Blue bird in the oak . . .
Woven in my word-song

White and slim my lover
Birch-tree in the shade
Mountain pools her fearless eyes
Innocent all-answering
Were I blinded to the Spring
Happy thrill would in me rise
Smiling half afraid
At the nearness of her

All my weak endeavor
Lay I at her feet
Like a moth from oversea
Let me longing lightly rest
On her flower petal breast
Till the red dawn set me free
To be with my sweet
Ever and forever . . .

* *Louise Bryant*

Index of titles of poems